HERE'S WHAT PEOPL]
POTENTIAL AND T

With passion and power, Troy calls readers to step forward out of the comfortable and recognize the potential God has placed inside each of our lives. *Potential* will speak straight to your heart and challenge you to live out the dreams that have been tucked away for far too long.

—*Randy Bezet*
Lead pastor, Bayside Community Church

Plenty of people talk about potential, but very few can actually reveal how to achieve it. But in *Potential: The Uncontainable Power of God Within You*, Troy Gramling has created a roadmap for discovering what you were put on the earth to accomplish and why it matters. Get this book. Don't spend another day without understanding your God-given potential, because once you do, it will change everything.

—*Phil Cooke, Ph.D.*
Filmmaker, media consultant
Author, *Maximize Your Influence*

Pastor Troy Gramling's newest book, *Potential: The Uncontainable Power of God Within You*, is a profound game-changer. With his authentic voice and relatable storytelling, you'll feel like you're sharing a heartfelt conversation with a trusted friend. Packed with real stories, raw truth, and practical insights, this book equips you to unleash the boundless potential of God within you. Trust me, this book will rock your world!

—*Havilah Cunnington*
Author, *Stronger Than the Struggle* and *Created to Hear God*

Potential. In my 1828 *Webster's Dictionary*, it means, "Any thing that is possible, but does not yet exist." One of the greatest gifts God will ever give you is *potential!* You have God-given potential. Perhaps there have been many sages throughout the ages who have written about potential. However, my friend Troy is not writing from a theoretical place but from an experiential life that has now given birth to the book you are holding in your hands. I believe that the level of your revelation determines the level of your transformation. *Potential* is not just another book, but it is a living, life-giving epistle that has been lived out and proven before there was one word ever written. I believe the greatest lifetime achievement you could ever attain would be to live your life to reach your full God-given potential—and now you have a *potential* map to help you do just that!

—*Keith A. Craft*
Founding pastor, Elevate Life Church; Think Coach

Troy Gramling's book is a very timely reminder that God has a brilliant plan for each of us. It is within our power to not only discover but unleash our potential and make a difference in this world. Pastor Troy offers an honest, informative, and often humorous guide to navigating challenging and difficult times on the path to bettering ourselves and our communities. There will be questions, obstacles, and setbacks, but with this invaluable resource at your side, there will be purpose, perseverance, and glory.

—*Tommy Barnett*
Global pastor, Dream City Church, Phoenix, AZ

If you want to discover the pathway that will unlock your potential, read this book! By authentically sharing his own journey, Troy helps each of us see the way to experience the potential of God in our own lives. This book will inspire you and help you take practical steps to experience the life God created you for.

—*Pastor Todd Mullins*
Christ Fellowship Church

All of us have an incredible amount of potential within us, a truth eloquently captured in *Potential: The Uncontainable Power of God Within You* by Pastor Troy Gramling. Our friendship has given me a firsthand view of Troy's deep understanding and commitment to nurturing the divine spark within each individual. His unique blend of personal anecdotes, pastoral wisdom, and scriptural insights provides a compelling roadmap for anyone seeking to unlock their God-given potential. This book is not just a reflection of Troy's profound spiritual journey but also a guiding light for those ready to explore the depths of their own capabilities. It's an honor to recommend a work that so powerfully conveys the transformative potential that lies within us all, penned by someone who has dedicated his life to helping others realize just that.

—*Jonathan Stockstill*
Pastor, Bethany Church, Baton Rouge, LA

Troy Gramling's new book *Potential* is a transformative journey unlocking the God-given potential within each of us. With profound insights and practical guidance, this book inspires and equips readers to fulfill their purpose. A must-read for those seeking personal growth and a deeper understanding of their unique path in life.

—*Dr. Dave Martin*
Best-selling author; America's #1 Christian success coach

Pastor Troy is as authentic as ever in his candid and powerful new book, *Potential*. A well-crafted, fun, yet thought-provoking ride, it proves why he is a master at leadership and communicating with others. Pastor Troy helps us discover and realize our unique potential to live our best life with God.

—*Gregg Avedon*
Owner, Avedon Essentials

Pastor Troy Gramling's *Potential: The Uncontainable Power of God Within You* offers remarkable encouragement to reflect, understand, and embrace God's given potential in us. His personal stories anchored on biblical principles take us on a journey of self-reflection and realization to unleash God's design and plan for us. The uncontainable power of God in us and through us is not a theory or wishful thinking. It is truth based on Scripture and demonstrated in Pastor Troy's life. This book truly inspires and challenges us to discover God's heart for His people and the ways we can genuinely experience God's best for our lives. May this book encourage you to pursue God's purpose for you!

—*Peter Tan-Chi*
Founder and senior pastor, Christ's Commission Fellowship

I have known Troy for more than fifteen years. He is an incredible person! You can't stand by Troy's side and not be inspired to live up to your full potential. I am so grateful to God for people like him in our life journey. You may often feel powerless and weak, but the truth in this book reminds you that God has already given you all you need to go through this life: He has given you potential. There is power within you that comes from God and is ready to be released for His glory. Troy's amazing story shows us that we too can face any challenge when we tap into our faith, authenticity, self-awareness, confidence, and so much more that is available to us. *Potential* will inspire you to start changing the world, beginning with yourself, right now! Remember, you were made just a little lower than the angels, as David said in Psalm 8. As the apostle Paul wrote to the Philippians, you can do all things through Him who strengthens you.

—*Carlito Paes*
Lead pastor, City Church, São Paulo, Brazil
Founder, Inspire Network of Churches

Potential is the book for anyone who feels the nudge toward a purpose and a calling, and yet is searching for how to take the first illuminated step and in what direction. Troy Gramling lays out the road map that equips and empowers the journeyman to embark with clarity and practical applications to stay on track. A must-read!

—*LoriAnn Biggers*
CEO, Triumph Capital Holdings
Co-host, *The Leader's Panel* podcast

Potential: The Uncontainable Power of God Within You is a phenomenal aid to all of us who constantly seek to live a meaningful and useful life. We all have the potential to leave a great legacy for the generation that will come after us. By discovering who we are and the gifts, talents, and dreams we have, and by cultivating an openness to change and a commitment to endure the challenges in this process, we will be ready to commit to the third element of Troy's proposed path: community. The community, the church in particular, provides the necessary support to unleash our potential in this generation and the generation after this, investing in those who will continue the journey we have begun. Wonderful and practical material indeed.

—*Elias Dantas*
Founder, Global Kingdom Partnership Network

It has been said that everyone is a pile of potential, and while that is true, it is also sadly true that not everyone unearths or discovers the potential with themselves. We all know the cemetery is full of unfulfilled dreams, unplayed songs. In writing this book *Potential*, Pastor Troy Gramling holds out the keys, the pick, and the shovel that will enable each one of us to unlock and unearth the gems that lie within. His honesty, openness, truthfulness, and vulnerability, which are laid out for all to see, tell us what kind of man Troy is—a man of sincerity and integrity. Let's be honest: any man who locks himself in a glass box for thirty days to break out of complacency and comfortability is a man who has something to say. And I must say huge kudos to his wife Stephanie; what a woman she is to stand by her man! Which again tells you something of their character. Nothing can beat life experience. Through this book, obviously full of potential itself, you may smile, laugh, and cry at some of the stories, but Troy's years of experience as a husband, father, friend, pastor, leader, and now author as well as a great human being shines through. In this well laid out, well thought out book, even each chapter title shows the building blocks for life. I heartily encourage everyone to pick up this very easy-to-read book and be inspired, be encouraged, and most of all discover some more of that God-given potential within you, the potential within that is dying to break out and help you fulfill your dreams. For truly, there is uncontainable power of God within you.

—*Peter Mortlock*
Founder, City Impact Churches International

Troy Gramling sounds a powerful alarm and sends a loud wake-up call in his new book, *Potential: The Uncontainable Power of God Within You*. Everyone has potential but for many of us, understanding how to tap into that potential has remained a mystery. That is until now. In this revealing book, Troy explains why this has been the case and shows us how to easily identify and unleash one of the greatest gifts God has given to us. He writes: "The fear of people finding out who you really are—seeing your insecurities, emotional pain, or personal failures—may be holding you back from realizing your true potential. But here is the good news: Even on the backside of the desert, you can't deny your destiny. God loves you too much to allow you to stay hidden forever. He knows your proficiency, your passion, your personality, and your past. He knows your potential!" If you know you're not where God wants you to be—that there's more He has called you to do—then this book is a must-read for you. Read it, digest it, and allow it to help unlock your God-given potential. I believe it will help you discover the real you and all God has placed inside you.

—*Henry Fernandez*
Senior pastor, The Faith Center, Sunrise, FL

Years ago when my dad died, I took over his church and tried to be just like him. As my dear friend Troy Gramling points out in his new book, trying to be somebody else *never* works. And it didn't work for me either. Trust me, revealing your authentic self can be kind of scary...but totally worth it. Pastor Troy's book will help you overcome your fears and insecurities and show you how to finally realize your amazing God-given potential.

—*David Crank*
Author, speaker, and lead pastor, FaithChurch.com

Potential is a master class in unlocking divine purpose, blending deep spiritual insights from Troy's personal journey of faith and leadership. Knowing Troy and his transformative ministry, I can attest to the life-changing power of his words. This book is an essential guide for anyone ready to step into their God-given potential. Troy's wisdom serves as a lighthouse, guiding the way to a life filled with extraordinary possibilities. Highly recommended for a journey of true self-discovery.

—*Terry Storch*
Co-founder, YouVersion

Troy Gramling is one of the few leaders who have consistently kept the main thing, the main thing. He has devoted his life to helping people develop their potential. His leadership, wisdom, and experience pour out onto the pages of this book. Prepare to be challenged, inspired, and activated.

—*Pastor Sergio De La Mora*
Founder, Cornerstone Church, San Diego

Pastor Troy Gramling gets right to the heart of what it takes to reach your God-given potential! With culture showing us how to hide behind our flaws, this book is an incredible read on how anyone can take a good look at themselves and see through the human façade. When you put these thoughts into action with God's guidance, you can fully become what you are created to be.

—*Terrell Somerville*
Founding pastor, Freedom Church, Gallatin, TN

I've known and watched Troy Gramling for over two decades now. His personal stories and powerful principles come at a great time to help you unleash your full potential. If you want a credible voice and practical principles to help you thrive in your next season, you picked the right book.

—*Stan Coleman*
Lead pastor, Prairie Valley Church, Campbell, TX

Pastor Tom Gramling has written a must-read for anyone who is seeking to reach their full potential in organizational leadership and beyond. In today's world, it is refreshing to find such a clear, concise, and well thought-out book. Pick up your copy today!

—*Wade Mumm, Ph.D.*
Senior pastor, Greeneway Church, Orlando, FL

Have you ever felt like you peaked or plateaued? Have you ever felt like there is more inside of you, and you can't seem to access it? It's time. As long as you're breathing, you have untapped potential. Pastor Troy Gramling's new book *Potential* will unlock the power within. Not hype, but a proven story and strategy to do it. The most powerful time in the universe is now. Take action and consume this book. Your confidence will change forever when you know all of heaven is cheering you on!

—*Buddy Cremeans*
Lead pastor, Northway Church, Clifton Park, NY

Potential is an inspiring and thought-provoking read! This book offers profound insights and practical wisdom for navigating life's challenges with faith and resilience. As a believer and friend of Pastor Troy, I highly recommend this book to anyone seeking spiritual guidance and a deeper understanding of their faith journey.

—*Alek Manoah*
Major League Baseball player

I've known Troy since we were thirteen years old! His baseball skills included a blistering fast ball, and he could dominate in basketball. There was always a special touch of God in everything he did. His book highlights his leadership abilities, and the hardships he faced in life enable him to guide others on their life journey. I truly enjoyed *Potential* and appreciate Troy's honesty!

—*Thax Turner*
Owner, Thax Turner & Co.

Everyone wants a blessing, but there is no blessing without a battle. The moment I declared to advance God's kingdom on earth further than all those who came before me, Satan unleashed his legion of demons. Unprepared for spiritual warfare, I literally lost billions of dollars. Know your enemy and choose your weapons wisely. Don't show up to a gunfight with a plastic knife. Troy Gramling's book *Potential* is your blueprint to unlock the supernatural power of God within you. Don't wage warfare without it!

—*Jack Owoc*
Former owner, Bang Energy

Potential is an inspiring and engaging read for those desiring to reach their God-given potential. Pastor Troy's journey and walk of faith will impact you no matter your vocation or stage of life.

—*Dave Divine*
Senior pastor, Chapelhill Church

How do I become the real, true authentic self I was created to be? Troy Gramling, a person I know to be humble and genuine, takes us on a wonderful journey to become the people we have the potential to be. He is raw and honest in his writing. And through his story, we discover our story. It's not magic. It's work, demanding that we be honest with ourselves to overcome our unique challenges. But the pages of *Potential* will set each of us free to become the person we have always wanted to be.

—*Mark Foreman*
Pastor emeritus, North Coast Calvary Chapel

I highly recommend Pastor Troy Gramling's new book *Potential*, which presents a unique look at how important it is to listen to that *still small voice*. Also important in Pastor Troy's development was his and Stephanie's ability and willingness to pivot from his dream of becoming a basketball coach to becoming a pastor. Of course, every good basketball player and coach knows how to pivot effectively!

—*Galen Avery*
AAA IT Services, Memphis

Pastor Troy Gramling has his finger on the pulse of today's leader. His years of experience, both professionally and spiritually, give him keen insight to speak into your life. In a world where Christ followers and leaders have become discouraged and disheartened through the generational challenges that we have faced in recent years, this book stirs faith that promotes action to regain our certainty as we recognize God's unlimited power in and through our lives.

—*Mark Merrill*
Lead pastor, Visalia First Assembly of God
Founder, Catalyst Bible College

Pastor Troy has allowed us to see the need to look beyond what we believe we are capable of and seek to live a life that unleashes the potential our Lord has created in us. He reminds us that we have all been called to more than we think or believe we are capable of. Thank you, Pastor Troy, for reminding me of the potential we have to change our world for Jesus!

—*John Whitehead*
Founder, JW Companies

Everyone has God-given potential, but how do we tap into it? If you know there's more in you, but you don't know where to start, Pastor Troy's new book, *Potential: The Uncontainable Power of God Within You*, will help you look within yourself while reaching to God for answers, finding the confidence you need to pursue your dreams. Be sure to make this book a part of your library!

—*Dr. James Davis*
President, Leadership Development International

POTENTIAL

TROY GRAMLING

THE UNCONTAINABLE POWER OF GOD WITHIN YOU

WHITAKER
HOUSE

POTENTIAL
The Uncontainable Power of God Within You

potentialchurch.com
www.facebook.com/potentialchurch
www.instagram.com/potentialchurch
www.youtube.com/potentialchurch

ISBN: 979-8-88769-216-6 • eBook ISBN: 979-8-88769-217-3
Printed in the United States of America
© 2024 by Troy Gramling

Whitaker House • 1030 Hunt Valley Circle • New Kensington, PA 15068
www.whitakerhouse.com

Library of Congress Cataloging-in-Publication Data
Names: Gramling, Troy, 1967- author.
Title: Potential : the uncontainable power of God within you / Troy
   Gramling.
Description: New Kensington, PA : Whitaker House, 2024. | Summary: "Using
   examples from the life of Moses, suggests that everyone has God-given
   potential within that enables them to pursue their dreams and discover
   their own promised land when they receive some coaching and
   encouragement"— Provided by publisher.
Identifiers: LCCN 2023053900 (print) | LCCN 2023053901 (ebook) | ISBN
   9798887692166 (trade paperback) | ISBN 9798887692173 (ebook)
Subjects: LCSH: Success—Religious aspects—Christianity. |
   Self-actualization (Psychology)—Biblical teaching. | Christian life. |
   BISAC: RELIGION / Christian Living / Calling & Vocation | SELF-HELP /
   Personal Growth / General
Classification: LCC BV4598.3 .G73 2024 (print) | LCC BV4598.3 (ebook) |
   DDC 248.4—dc23/eng/20240221
LC record available at https://lccn.loc.gov/2023053900
LC ebook record available at https://lccn.loc.gov/2023053901

1 2 3 4 5 6 7 8 9 10 11   ⊔⊔   31 30 29 28 27 26 25 24

DEDICATION

This book is dedicated to those who have believed in me and God's call upon my life, beginning with Stephanie, my beloved, who with one look can inspire me to reach for the stars, whose support never waivers, and who I love with every ounce and fiber of my being. Her encouragement for the last thirty-five years made this book possible.

I am also thankful for the constant cheerleading of our three children and their spouses—Tyler (Amber); Carson (Jessica); and Baylee (Larry)—as well as Lyon and Luna, the best grandkids in the world, who are on their own journey to reach their potential; my dad and mom, Jim Gramling and Linda Porter, who have always told me to never give up; my brothers, Mark and Jimmy Gramling, who daily challenged me and made me better; and my in-laws, Mike and Betty Cox, whose example and courage have been steadfast.

This book is also dedicated to: Jackie and Mary May, who saw something very early in Steph and me and have cultivated it to this day; Mario Padrino and Raul Palacios, who wouldn't let me surrender my potential at one of the lowest times in my life; Pastor Dan Southerland, who gave me an opportunity; Pastor Matt Jacobs, who believed in the principles enough to get the ball rolling and literally gave me no choice but to *just do it*; Yissel Munoz, who has worked tirelessly to get this story into many people's hands; Pastor Danny Fernandez, who continually encouraged me; Dr. James Davis, whose help has been indispensable; and the Potential Church team and congregation, who have believed in Stephanie and me for twenty-four years. They have loved, followed, encouraged, and partnered with our family to reach our potential. Thank you to these and so many others. I truly love you!

CONTENTS

STEP THREE: COMMUNITY

FOREWORD

Some pastors are gifted communicators and thrive when it comes to feeding their congregations. Some pastors are strong leaders, casting vision and wielding a great amount of influence. Very rarely do you find people who are gifted communicators *and* leaders, but Pastor Troy Gramling is one such man.

If you've ever had the notion that great leaders have all the answers, never get things wrong, and never have any fear, you're about to read some stories from Pastor Troy that might surprise you. The truth is, great leaders sometimes struggle to know exactly what to do next, and mistakes are inevitable. And if you think leaders are fearless, that simply isn't true. However, as Pastor Troy authentically and transparently points out, one thing that sets great leaders apart is they refuse to settle for *good* when they believe they can have *great*.

That's how he has operated for more than two decades leading Potential Church near Miami, Florida, and pastoring churches in Arkansas years prior. Like every leader, he has experienced several setbacks, but the way he has picked himself up after being knocked down is motivating and inspiring. He calls it failing forward, and he uses Scripture to back up this principle.

Throughout this book, Pastor Troy parallels his leadership guidance with the story of the Israelites leaving Egypt and wandering through the desert. With Moses as their leader, and later Joshua, the people of Israel traveled to the promised land. From this well-known story, Pastor Troy shares proven leadership principles he has applied to his own life.

Pastor Troy also shares that "Good leadership isn't what happens when you're around; it's what happens when you're *not there*." In other words, you can see the proof of your good leadership when your vision continues successfully when you're not around. You can see this play out in Deuteronomy 31–34, when Joshua took over for Moses and became the leader as the children of Israel traveled into the promised land. As you might know, Moses died before the end of the journey, but in Joshua's capable hands, the Israelites reached their God-ordained destination. And while Moses never reached the promised land, Joshua's success reflected Moses's leadership.

I've thought about this concept quite a bit over the last few years as I plan to transition the senior pastor role to my son James. Like Joshua taking the baton from Moses and continuing to lead the Israelites, I believe our church will be in capable hands because James reflects my leadership and is committed to following the Lord's vision for Gateway Church.

Leading people isn't always easy, and overcoming moments of fear requires great faith. With every victory, there may also be missteps, mistakes, and failures along the way. I love what God said to Joshua when he was set in place to lead the Jews: *"Have I not commanded you? Be strong and of good courage; do not be afraid, nor be dismayed, for the LORD your God is with you wherever you go"* (Joshua 1:9 NKJV).

As you read this book, Pastor Troy will challenge and encourage you to overcome fear, recover from mistakes gracefully, and fail forward. And he will give you the knowledge and tools you need to do it all well. This book will help you dig deeper to reach your potential and be all God created you to be!

—*Robert Morris*
Senior pastor, Gateway Church
Best-selling author, *The Blessed Life*,
The God I Never Knew, and *Grace, Period*

PREFACE

I will always remember the day when I trusted Christ. I was a shy, nine-year-old kid sitting next to my mom at a revival at Calvary Baptist Church in Paragould, Arkansas. I might have nodded on other Sundays when the preacher asked me if I was saved. But on this Sunday, I heard Christ's voice whispering, "Trust Me," and I was truly convicted.

Since that day, I can't remember a time when Christ has called me to do something, and I haven't done it. Oh, I'm not perfect. There have been times when I've rebelled or dragged my heels and not followed His directions immediately. But eventually, I'm humbled and get back on the path.

Writing this book has been a journey. It's something that I've known God has wanted me to do. In some sense, I've been disobedient; I have known it for a decade, yet I've wrestled with it. I've been a pastor for nearly thirty years, so I feel confident in what God has given me to say aloud. But to sit down and write a book? I was admittedly afraid. I knew God wanted me to use the written word, but I wasn't quite sure why. Honestly, part of me just wanted to finish this book so I could say, "I did it, God! Let's move on to the next thing!"

For me, it always comes back to the word *potential*. When we began the process in 2010 to change the name of our church here in Florida from Flamingo Road Church—as it had been known for thirty years—it was a practical decision. If we were going to have multiple sites, in cities and countries where it's hard to grow churches, having a large pink bird as our mascot wasn't going to work. But the name change became much more than that.

I believe that God calls certain people at a certain time to a certain place. I knew that God sent me and my wife Stephanie to this church from our home in Arkansas to help people connect to their *potential*—not just to better themselves but to change the world for good. The name Potential Church seemed perfect.

Just to be safe, I checked that the online handles—domain name, Twitter, Facebook, etc.—for "Potential" were still available. I was shocked to see that they all were. *Potential* is not an uncommon word, but it's a powerful one. To declare that you are going to help others manifest their God-given potential is perhaps more than most people, churches, or businesses want to promise. We looked for a name to wholly represent a thought, a calling, and a message. I've got to believe that seeing someone wearing a "Potential Church" T-shirt inspires others to enter our doors.

I finished the first two chapters of *Potential* in early 2020, intending to take them with me to Rome, Italy, for an international convention of pastors. I was nervous but excited to share my words of wisdom with my peers and mentors.

Little did I know that I had a whole lot of learnin' to do before the rest of this book would be completed. I probably don't have to tell you that the trip to Italy didn't happen. The COVID-19 pandemic was a crisis of a magnitude that this world had not experienced in modern times. Every day, I struggled with the latest challenge. Potential Church's doors shut, schools closed, and my adult children moved in with me. I preached and held prayer groups online and even conducted virtual funeral services. Months passed, and my early manuscript lay untouched. I was too busy struggling to keep my family, staff, and followers healthy in mind and body. I didn't always succeed. My faith—and perhaps yours too—was tested in ways it never had been before. Many nights, I laid in bed unable to sleep and prayed to God that people would not give in to despair or think that He had abandoned them.

Life is not just about merely existing. God has a brilliant plan for each of us from the beginning; we just have to connect to it. The hungry *will* be fed. There *will* be peace instead of brokenness and pain. But if you lose God, you lose that sense of purpose, that potential.

Writing a book is not for the faint of heart. Neither is *reading* this book! But after the various crises we have all endured up to this point, let's not go back to life as usual. Let's not go back to our routines. I have learned more in the last few years than I did in thirty years of pastoring, and I have sought to convey those powerful lessons here in these pages. This unprecedented time—which has stripped down our values, needs, and beliefs to their very essence—calls us to step forward with a renewed commitment to uncover and unleash the potential that God Himself has bestowed on each and every one of us.

Potential *is* the uncontainable power of God within you. You only need to cooperate.

In Christ,
Troy Gramling

INTRODUCTION

I dedicated this book to her a few pages earlier but let me just say it again: *I have the best wife in the world.*

More than thirty years ago, Stephanie and I stood in our tiny kitchen in Paragould, Arkansas, a space that was too small for the two of us—well, too small for six feet four inches of me and literally anyone else. It was 1990. Steph and I were still practically newlyweds. We were both just about to finish college with degrees in education. We planned to become teachers, and I was also going to coach basketball. We had a little apartment, did what we needed to get by, and talked about having kids. Our family and friends were all just a few miles away. Everything was going great, all according to plan.

Except for one thing: I had a secret to share with Stephanie.

I had grown up in church—my mom made sure my two brothers and I were there every Sunday—and I always enjoyed children's church and youth group. So when the little country church that Steph and I attended asked if we would volunteer to teach a Sunday school class, we said yes. We had *no idea* how to do it, but we bought a few books at the Christian bookstore, did some reading, and gave it our best shot.

FEELING THE NUDGE FROM GOD

As we prepared each week's lesson, something began to change in me. I had never thought for a second about a career in ministry; I didn't even know what that meant. But I began to feel a *nudge* within me. At first, I just brushed it aside, thinking to myself, "No way!" I loved basketball and coaching. That's why I went to college—to teach and coach basketball.

But with every Sunday school lesson, I became more confident that something inside me had changed. Finally, I realized I had to share this with Steph. So one night, standing at the kitchen counter, I opened my mouth and just blurted it out: "I think I'm being called into the ministry."

I could see Steph's confusion. Where was this coming from? The tension was high in that tiny kitchen!

That nudge I felt more than thirty years ago was my first acknowledgment of the power of my potential. As it turned out, casting my vision for a life in ministry was not as straightforward as teaching a math class. I was used to showing students a step-by-step procedure on the chalkboard, which then led to a definite solution. I would have had a hard time sketching out my future plans in chalk for Steph! But I had taken the first step.

To achieve your goals in life, to answer the calling that is uniquely yours, takes *potential*.

Now I could have ignored that dream and taken a high school teaching and coaching job. I could have watered it down and continued to teach Sunday school. While I wasn't clear on exactly what the future would look like—whether it meant a student ministry or pastoring an entire church—I was certain it *didn't* mean coaching high school basketball.

So I turned down the coaching job I had been offered. When presented with the exact achievement I had always dreamed about, I said no. It wasn't that I had another job; I didn't! After graduation, Steph and I were still volunteering at that little country church. By this time, Steph had not only accepted but embraced what God had called us both to do. We were working part-time jobs, and I was substitute teaching. You read that right. I had turned down a coaching job, only to find myself providing for my family by *substitute teaching!*

Why didn't I just take the coaching job?

It stemmed out of my confidence that I knew what *wasn't* my future. I was afraid that if I said yes, I would get trapped and never pursue what I knew God was calling me to do. There was a price to pay for that decision: working two jobs, late nights, weekends, and living in a sense of limbo about what the future held.

I am grateful every day that Steph chose to trust my vision. It took us a few years to steady ourselves, years that we could have been already living on two teachers' salaries, buying a house, and starting a family. In fact, our quality of life took a dip before it took an upswing.

SOMETHING GREATER AWAITS!

Whether you're just starting out like I was or you're well into building your career and family, if you feel that *nudge* toward something greater, *this book is for you.* As long as your heart beats and your lungs take in air, there is time! God hasn't given up on you or His dream for you. Embracing your faults, giving up trying to be something that you are not, accepting that you have strengths and weaknesses—these realizations free you up to achieve your unique God-given potential!

But you can't go where you want to go unless you first understand where you're at. Therefore, the first four chapters of *Potential* are devoted to self-discovery. We will use powerful tools of self-awareness and self-examination to understand what you are truly capable of, so you can give voice to your vision with confidence.

The second part of *Potential* discusses the challenges you will inevitably meet along the way. Maybe this is where you've found yourself stalling before—you've taken steps toward your dreams but lost your nerve. Well, this time, I will help you to understand that if the road seems long and winding, you are going the right way! Nothing that comes easily is the real thing.

The third and final section of *Potential* is devoted to community. You will need help on the path to realize your potential, and the people who reveal themselves as your supporters may surprise you. As you rise, you help others to do the same. That is the ultimate success!

OUR COMPANIONS: MOSES AND GOD

We have two important companions on this journey. The first is Moses. From being cast down the river as an infant to life in Pharaoh's palace, from killing a man to exile in the desert, and finally being called by God at the age of eighty to lead His chosen people out of slavery in Egypt, Moses's story is full of lessons on what to do and what *not* to do on the road to our potential. Moses is flawed, hasty, impatient, and self-doubting, but he is also loyal, selfless, devout, and humble. In other words, he is deeply *human*, and he is the perfect example for us.

The second and most important companion is God Himself. Even though you may question or disappoint Him along the way, He will never leave your side. When God appeared to Moses in the form of a burning bush in all His glory, to ask him to answer the calling he was born to do and lead His people out of Egypt, Moses basically answered, "I'm not up to the task. Isn't there someone else?" (See Exodus 3:11–13; 4:1–13.) I still shake my head in disbelief when I think about it!

Reflecting on your own story up to this point in your life, do you find yourself answering God's call in the same way? Do you feel that nudge that you were born to greatness, but you can't get out of your own way? Do you tell yourself there must be someone else more talented, more confident, knowledgeable, better looking, or smarter?

I don't blame you for having doubts. It's taken me twenty years to sit down and write this book. But I am here to tell you that once I picked up my pen, God picked *me* up again and again.

I'm not saying it was easy! Not only was writing this book a challenge, but as I began, the world was hit with the COVID-19 shutdown. Potential Church shut its doors, as did other churches, and my staff and I had to pivot entirely to serve our congregation, hold services and school online, organize food drives, minister to the sick—the changes seemed endless.

At long last, when it seemed like the world was coming out of the pandemic crisis and I put the finishing touches on *Potential*, I was hospitalized with a life-threatening case of COVID...and then so were my family members. I thought, "What if I never get out of this hospital bed and never complete this book?" I prayed to the Lord to help me do both, and the copy you hold in your hands is proof that He graciously brought both prayers to fruition.

I'll spare you the suspense. I am not perfect, and neither are you. But you and I can do amazing things with the Lord's help, and our example of faith in Him and perseverance will inspire others. I have relied on the power of potential for my entire adult life, and I invite you to start to do so as well!

STEP ONE:
SELF-DISCOVERY

1

THE POWER OF AUTHENTICITY: REVEALING YOUR POTENTIAL

Are you living life with integrity or hiding
on the backside of the desert?

In 2017, my wife and I spent a month in a 10-by-20-foot glass house beside Potential Church in Fort Lauderdale, Florida. For thirty days, four cameras recorded every move we made, day and night, and streamed it live on the church website. (Thankfully, we were not on camera while we changed our clothes or used the restroom!) It wasn't long before I, the "Naked Pastor," went viral on Twitter and got some attention in the newspaper and on television.

This seemingly crazy act was in conjunction with a sermon series I called "Naked and NOT Afraid," devoted to the subject of authenticity. I had gotten the idea from the popular Discovery Channel reality series *Naked and Afraid,*[1] a survival show that deposits two total strangers, usually a man and a woman, in a dangerous wilderness with no clothes, food,

---

1. *Naked and Afraid*. Produced by David Garfinkle. Discovery Channel, 2013–present.

or water for twenty-one days. Keep in mind that there is no prize for doing this—no million dollars, no new car, not even a box of protein bars. If they complete the challenge (and many do not), these adventure-seekers emerge with nothing but their pride, a sense of accomplishment, and an overwhelming need for a shower.

NOWHERE TO HIDE

While Stephanie and I didn't remove our clothes on camera, living in a glass house day and night for thirty days certainly left us feeling exposed. There was literally no place to hide. We slept on a Murphy bed, cooked meals in a toaster oven, and conducted church business in a 200-square-foot glass box. What we discussed was heard, and what we did was seen.

Now the question you might be asking yourself is, "Pastor Troy, what the heck were you thinking?" Trust me, it's the first question I got from Steph when I mentioned the idea!

But the truth is, prior to this time, I had been feeling uneasy for a while. I had gotten to a comfortable place. It wasn't perfect, but it certainly wasn't terrible either. I had been lead pastor at Potential Church for more than fourteen years, the congregation was growing, my kids were healthy, and for the first time, we actually had a few dollars saved. Everything seemed to be fine, but deep down, I knew I was capable of more. I knew that I would have to do something drastic to disrupt my comfort level, invigorate my potential, and understand how to live it out. If I was going to be the pastor of a church called Potential, then I'd better intentionally strive to activate my own!

I thought of Moses on the backside of the desert. There he was, born to greatness, the man who would be called to lead the Israelites, God's chosen people, out of slavery—and he was working as a shepherd! The only creatures he was leading anywhere were sheep. And not only that, he was eighty years old! I am writing these words at age fifty-five, a decade older than Moses was when he fled into the desert in exile. Moses had his family and friends around him; his gig was humble but solid. Everything on the surface was fine—as it was for me.

But like Moses, I knew that I too had to search for greener pastures. Like Moses, in the middle of the night, when everything was quiet, I looked around and thought, "Is this all there is? Big buildings, parking lots, state-of-the-art technology?" Or was it about the people and the hundreds of flickering lights in the homes I could see from our church campus?

Was I also going to wait until I was eighty to realize my true calling?

GOD WANTS YOU TO BE YOU

To fully reveal yourself, to be your authentic self, is one of God's purposes for you. It has been part of our covenant with the Lord since day six of creation, when God created man. God wants us to understand that this was His intention. It's so integral to human experience that He put it right in Genesis, in the first pages of the Bible. When Adam and Eve do the one thing God has told them not to do—eat the fruit of the Tree of Knowledge of Good and Evil—they feel shame. They realize they are naked; they have failed. But instead of confessing their sins and asking for God's forgiveness, they run and hide. Adam says, "*So I hid. I was afraid because I was naked*" (Genesis 3:10).

Let's remember why Moses was cuddling up to sheep in the first place. Like Adam and Eve, he failed to trust in the Lord's plan and tried to hide it. Moses also failed big time in most people's eyes, including his own—and he was found out. Scripture states:

> *Moses…went out to visit his own people, the Hebrews, and he saw how hard they were forced to work. During his visit, he saw an Egyptian beating one of his fellow Hebrews. After looking in all directions to make sure no one was watching, Moses killed the Egyptian and hid the body in the sand. The next day, when Moses went out to visit his people again, he saw two Hebrew men fighting. "Why are you beating up your friend?" Moses said to the one who had started the fight. The*

> *man replied, "Who appointed you to be our prince and judge? Are you*
> *going to kill me as you killed that Egyptian yesterday?"*
>
> (Exodus 2:11–14)

Does this sound like the man who would lead God's people to freedom—a man who committed murder, hid the body, then fled to the far-off land of Midian to escape Pharaoh's death penalty? Midian was a desert wilderness region in the middle of nowhere.

When Moses was confronted with who he was, he ran. He found himself on the backside of the desert, all to hide from God, his own people, and his responsibilities. But Moses wasn't the first person in Scripture, nor the last person on earth, to feel naked and afraid.

Why are we so quick to run and hide? What is it about failure that keeps us from admitting it and experiencing forgiveness? Why are we afraid to be naked emotionally, personally, and professionally? What makes *authenticity* such a scary word?

Why do we continue to avoid living in a figurative glass house? When Steph and I were living in a real one, there were times when a storm would threaten to blow that little structure down. The rain would pound, the winds would howl, and the roof would leak. But every time a storm came, I would pick up the phone, and in a matter of minutes, a team of pastors and volunteers would show up to help us through the tempest.

By picking up this book, you too are inviting a team of people into your life to keep the coming storms from destroying your dreams.

FROM THE GARDEN THROUGH THE DESERT TO YOUR DESTINY

The fear of people finding out who you really are—seeing your insecurities, emotional pain, or personal failures—may be holding you back from realizing your true potential.

But here is the good news: Even on the backside of the desert, you can't deny your destiny. God loves you too much to allow you to stay hidden forever. He knows your proficiency, your passion, your personality, and your past. He knows your potential!

After He banished Adam and Eve from the garden of Eden, God made tunics out of animal skins for them. He stayed in their lives and those of their children. Adam and Eve failed, but God didn't give up on them or His plan for them. He replaced their guilt with forgiveness. He disciplined them, telling Eve, *"I will sharpen the pain of your pregnancy, and in pain you will give birth,"* and telling Adam, *"By the sweat of your brow will you have food to eat"* (Genesis 3:16, 19). But He also promised them that they would be part of humanity's redemption. (See Genesis 3:15.) That's a pretty big opportunity for the two people who were the first to disobey God and bring sin and evil into the world!

Moses learned of his big opportunity to achieve his potential when he discovered God on the backside of the desert:

> *One day Moses was tending the flock of his father-in-law, Jethro, the priest of Midian. He led the flock far into the wilderness and came to Sinai, the mountain of God. There the angel of the LORD appeared to him in a blazing fire from the middle of a bush. Moses stared in amazement.* (Exodus 3:1–2)

I believe that Moses's amazement had more to do with the realization that God was pursuing him than it did with His appearance in a burning bush.

God is also pursuing you. The fact that you picked up *Potential* out of thousands of books and find yourself reading this very page is a challenge to move beyond your fears and failures and embrace *your* potential.

God assured Moses that failure is not final, that he had potential for a specific task:

> *Now go, for I am sending you to Pharaoh. You must lead my people Israel out of Egypt.* (Exodus 3:10)

While God spoke to Moses through a burning bush, He wants to speak to you through His Word:

Don't be afraid, for I am with you. Don't be discouraged, for I am your God. I will strengthen you and help you. I will hold you up with my victorious right hand. (Isaiah 41:10)

MY BURNING BUSH: I GOT FIRED

I'm only human. I waited until the last few pages of this chapter to share with you what I once saw as my biggest crisis of faith.

Twenty years ago, after fifteen years of church leadership, Steph and I moved from our hometown of Paragould, Arkansas, to Little Rock to plant a church. We were encouraged and challenged to move by our denominational leadership. They promised their financial support, mentorship, and assistance to get the new project off the ground.

But once we arrived in Little Rock, their attitudes began to change. They questioned our strategy, our team members, and our timetable. After only three months there, instead of the help I was promised, I received a phone call from the denominational leader. He said the church plant project was "a hot potato"—and he was dropping it.

It was that quick and that cold. I was flabbergasted. How could they fire me after I had moved my whole family to a new city, put my kids into a new school, and taken a second job to help support the church? But they did! I felt fear, frustration, and embarrassment. I was naked and afraid. What would I tell my wife and kids? How could I face the folks who believed in me? Would everyone see me as a failure? Everything in me wanted to run and hide!

Then, from the burning bush of God's Word, I heard this prophetic proclamation: *"Do not gloat over me, my enemies! For though I fall, I will rise again"* (Micah 7:8).

A BIGGER, BETTER DREAM

It's been twenty years since I received that phone call, and God has taken our family on an incredible journey. The dream I had in Little Rock was way too small for all that God had planned. It has allowed us to pastor a church with more members than the population of Paragould. We have partnered with dozens of church planters from around the world. We have a thriving multimedia ministry, including TV, online, and print. And while the COVID-19 pandemic sidelined many ministries, God used it to expand our influence in our community and around the world. The fact that I had experienced *failure* twenty years ago and didn't surrender the dream gave me the strength needed in these current challenging times to take risks and partner with people to experience *their* potential.

Although I was afraid of failure, that was the very thing God used to propel me into my potential. Along the way, I learned that God uses the Troy He created, not the one I might pretend to be. It's when I'm willing to be honest about my insecurities, my emotional pain, and even my personal failures that God can heal and forgive. And as I learned while living in a glass house, authenticity is challenging but worth the effort.

In his book *Getting Naked: A Business Fable About Shedding the Three Fears that Sabotage Client Loyalty*, popular business consultant and writer Patrick Lencioni speaks about "humble self-confidence":

Even though clients require us to be competent enough to meet their needs, it is ultimately our honesty, humility, and selflessness that will endear us to them and allow them to trust and depend on us.[2]

I believe this quote applies not only to business relationships, but also to how I serve my wife, family, friends, colleagues, and my congregants at Potential Church.

Be humble but be confident that *you* have been chosen by God to realize a divine potential intended just for you.

---

2. Patrick M. Lencioni, *Getting Naked: A Business Fable About Shedding the Three Fears That Sabotage Client Loyalty* (New York: John Wiley & Sons, 2010).

Living in a glass house, I realized that even when we discover *who* we are and the potential we have for greatness, we can still struggle to be authentic. Being naked before the world is extremely frightening, even *with* our clothes on, but in order to be successful in life, we must be our real selves. As Steph and I discovered, it's not always easy. Being genuine can be uncomfortable because we feel so exposed.

Living in a time of cancel culture has upped the stakes on failure. Those who express doubt, provoke conversation, or ask questions risk being criticized, fired, or even harmed. But why do we fear being authentic, appearing vulnerable, and admitting our mistakes? They're all part of being human and usually provide the perfect opportunity to change, to rise. As Ford Motor Company founder Henry Ford once said, "Failure is simply the opportunity to begin again, this time more intelligently."

Are you living an authentic life or hiding somewhere on the backside of the desert? Stop running from your past. It's time that you were naked and *not* afraid. And I have great news for you: you can keep your clothes on! In the next three chapters, we're going to step toward your divinely given potential together.

QUESTIONS FOR REFLECTION

Do you ever wonder if you, like Moses, are going to have to wait until you are eighty years old to realize your true calling?

What do you love to do so much that you would be willing to pay to do it?

When was the last time you challenged your comfort zone, or disrupted your normal routine, schedule, or thoughts with a new action or perspective?

Henry Ford said, "Failure is simply the opportunity to begin again, this time more intelligently." Can you think of a time in your life when a failure or admitting that you felt unsure or vulnerable turned out to be a blessing in disguise?

2

THE POWER OF REFLECTION: A GOOD LOOK IN THE MIRROR

Wishing, praying, or trying to be somebody else won't work.
Your potential is yours alone.

There have been times when I've wanted to be someone else—an extrovert instead of an introvert, a basketball coach rather than a pastor, or Joel Osteen instead of Troy Gramling. In fifth grade, all the girls thought Scott Baio from the TV series *Happy Days* was a *hunk*, so every night, I tucked a photo of him under my pillow, praying to God that I would wake up looking just like him. But to my disappointment (and to that of the girls in my class, I'm sure), every morning when I rushed to the mirror, instead of a teen heartthrob, there I was: Troy Gramling.

My guess is that there have also been times in your life when you've wished, prayed, or even tried to be someone else, anybody other than who you are.

You and I are not alone. Moses had the same kind of insecure thoughts, despite being chosen by God to lead His people out of slavery and into the promised land, their destiny.

MOSES ALSO HAD DOUBTS

When God told Moses that he had been chosen for such an extraordinary adventure, his response wasn't one of excitement or confidence. He replied, *"Who am I to appear before Pharaoh? Who am I to lead the people of Israel out of Egypt?"* (Exodus 3:11).

In fact, Moses needed quite a bit of convincing that he was up to this challenge. Remember, he was eighty years old, but life was good. He was surrounded by family, enjoyed regular meals, and had a flock of sheep that probably listened to him and followed him anywhere. True, he was in the desert, not the promised land, but it was comfortable enough. He protested further:

> *If I go to the people of Israel and tell them, "The God of your ancestors has sent me to you," they will ask me, "What is his name?" Then what should I tell them?* (Exodus 3:13)

God was also quick to let Moses know that this journey wasn't one that he would have to travel alone, especially given the intimidating task of telling the people that God had sent him. In every moment, He promised to be right beside him. (See Exodus 4:12.)

Moses continued to hesitate. He asked, *"What if they won't believe me or listen to me?"* (Exodus 4:1). *"Then the LORD asked him, "What is that in your hand?"* (verse 2). God then gave Moses the ability to turn his shepherd's staff into a serpent and back into a staff again. God also had Moses slip his hand under his robe; it came out leprous and covered in boils. But after another pass, his hand was restored to health! Moses literally had the tools that he needed to lead the people in his hands. God told Moses that these two miraculous signs would convince the people—and if not, Moses could take some water from the Nile and pour it on the ground, where it would turn to blood as further proof that Moses had been sent by God. (See Exodus 4:8–9.)

WHAT IS IN YOUR HAND?

Rather than focus on what you don't have, what you can't do, or who you aren't, why not ask, "What's in *my* hand?" What gifts do you have? What are you passionate about? Where have you been? These questions will lead you to unleash what you already have in your hand—your unique *potential, the uncontainable power of God within you.*

Just like Moses, you were created for something more than you are experiencing right now. But perhaps you're struggling to keep your head above water, so you too may be asking, "Who am I?"

We read about greatness as we scroll through stories of heroism on Instagram or Facebook. We think to ourselves, "I could never do that." We believe that heroes are different, that they don't have the same problems or struggles that we wrestle with on a daily basis. They must have more money or a better education. There must be *something* special about them.

But is that true? Moses overcame his fear. He discovered that the elusive *something* he needed was already in his hand. Gradually, he understood his potential through the provision of God. And you can do the same!

CHOOSE YOUR SELF-PRESENTATIONS CAREFULLY,
FOR WHAT STARTS OUT AS A MASK
MAY BECOME YOUR FACE.
—ERVING GOFFMAN

THREE AREAS THAT MAKE US HIDE

Let's look at three areas in our life that can make even the strongest among us look for a good hiding place.

SELF-IMAGE

Do you look in the mirror sometimes and see only flaws? Do you ever wonder why you don't get as many likes as that influencer on Instagram, close blockbuster deals like your boss, bake lasagna as good as your mom, or shoot hoops like that hustler at the Saturday night pickup game?

I can relate. Twenty years ago, I went from serving as lead pastor at a church in a little town in Arkansas to serving as the parking attendant at a megachurch just thirty miles from Miami.

Yes, you read that right. When I came to Potential—then named Flamingo Road Church—Lead Pastor Dan Southerland had been at the church for ten years and had built it up from just a few congregants to a few thousand. He invited me to come to Fort Lauderdale and start a young adult ministry. But leading a ministry that was only in the planning stages left me free on Sundays—and the biggest need on Sunday was showing people where to park. So most congregants first got to know me as the tall guy who waved a flag at their cars in the parking lot on Sunday.

Pastor Dan was amazing. I studied him every minute I got. A natural extrovert, he would walk into a room and totally own it. He smoked cigars. He had a big grandfatherly smile and a booming voice. He looked like he could hold his own with Joel Osteen and Rick Warren—and he did. They were his colleagues. He was a polished, self-confident leader.

I had been a college basketball player, so I was most comfortable in Air Jordans and jeans. I had tattoos, and I had not seen a lot of those in the church rows on Sundays. With my quiet voice and Arkansas accent, I was more comfortable in small groups than commanding a room. When Dan offered me a cigar one night, I had no idea how to light it. I had a lot to learn! That's why I was in the parking lot showing people where to park. I had a *whatever it takes* mindset, and I was a sponge for whatever the pastor and his congregation had to teach me.

FROM PARKING LOT TO PASTOR

At the time, Pastor Dan had just written a successful book called *Transitioning*, and he began traveling to help other churches transition for growth. In his absence, I was given the opportunity to speak occasionally. Then after just a year, Dan took me to lunch and shared that he was going on the road permanently to speak and teach. He and his family were moving to North Carolina, and he was going to recommend me to become lead pastor at Flamingo Road Church. As this unfolded, in the eyes of most people, the parking attendant had just become lead pastor!

While Dan lived in North Carolina, he returned to Florida once a month to preach at a church right down the road. People love their pastor. And the fact that they could drive a few miles further and see him once a month wasn't wasted on many of them. We had small and large groups of people leave to go down the street. While it wasn't the intention of Pastor Dan or the other church to take our congregants, it was happening, and I was going to have to deal with it.

"How am I going to keep them here?" I thought. "Should I start acting like their former pastor? Put on a suit like Joel Osteen? A Hawaiian shirt like Rick Warren?" I felt insecure. I was tempted to change myself, to model myself externally after these successful pastors. Inauthenticity may feel right at first...until it gets revealed. Wearing that Joel Osteen suit may have fooled my congregation for a few weeks, but eventually, they would have seen me itching and sweating!

God has created each and every one of us for our own special greatness. As David declares to God:

> *You made all the delicate, inner parts of my body and knit me together in my mother's womb. Thank you for making me so wonderfully complex! Your workmanship is marvelous.*   (Psalm 139:13–14)

I decided that instead of chasing the personas of these other successful pastors, I was going to be as authentic as possible. I'd keep the sneakers and not cover up my tattoos. I'd speak in my normal voice, with my Southern accent. And as often as possible, I would meet with people in breakout groups and other small gatherings so we could have casual conversations and get to know each other better. In essence, I decided to be as comfortable as possible in my own skin. Rather than becoming something I wasn't, I would embrace who I was. We focused on ministering to the community and became more diverse and intentionally multicultural. No suits or flowery shirts—but we might keep the cigars!

YOUR TIME IS LIMITED,
SO DON'T WASTE IT LIVING SOMEONE ELSE'S LIFE.
—STEVE JOBS

EMOTIONAL PAIN

"Are you okay?"

We are often asked this question when others think something is wrong with us—and we try to reassure them by responding, "I'm fine."

But is that an honest response?

I have been a pastor for more than twenty-five years, and there have been many late nights when my heart and soul hurt. When someone I loved did something I didn't understand. When someone I spent hours supporting just walked away. And worst of all, when those I have laughed with, ministered with, and walked the path of life with said things about me that were just not true.

Church folks are people just like everyone else and that includes church staff teams. It is our *people-ness* that causes the pain. Amid the COVID-19 shutdown, like many organizations, we had to cut back. At times, we lowered executive teams' salaries and halted plans that had been in motion for years. But we worked very hard to make sure that the staff were able to stay employed. My wife and I felt strongly and prayed earnestly to make this happen, for months carrying the weight of their having the capacity to provide for their families.

So it was tough when we found out that while we were working so hard to keep everyone employed, some of our staff members were quietly looking for *other opportunities*. I have always supported staff pursuing their best opportunity to reach their potential, but when it's pursued secretly, it feels like betrayal and a lack of loyalty, even when it's unintentional. And it can be difficult to trust again.

It doesn't matter whether it is the result of something you did, something someone else did, or something you just don't understand—the reality is that emotional pain *hurts*. Divorce, job loss, estrangement from family, the loss of a friend, and countless other real events lead to heartache. No one is safe from its grasp, and the grief is like a wave that pounds the shore over and over.

HIDING THE PAIN

Yet when someone asks me if I'm okay, I still find myself unwilling to give an honest answer. When we are in pain, choosing to be authentic and admitting how we feel just takes too much energy and time—or so we believe.

As a pastor, I should know better. I see people try to hide their pain, or at least numb it, using Netflix, social media, or the old standbys—drugs, sex, and alcohol.

THE BEST ANTIDOTE FOR LONELINESS,
HOPELESSNESS, AND FEAR IS VULNERABILITY:
SHARING YOUR SECRETS AND TALKING ABOUT
WHAT SHAMES YOU, WHAT YOU FEAR.
—JEWEL

It's hard to deal with emotional pain. Rather than walk through the hurt, we are often lured into trying anything to hide it and escape from reality. It's easier to pretend or self-medicate than it is to admit that we've been wounded for fear of appearing to be weak.

But there is some comfort in knowing that God is never closer to us than when we are in pain:

You keep track of all my sorrows. You have collected all my tears in your bottle...This I know: God is on my side. (Psalm 56:8–9)

The LORD is close to the brokenhearted; he rescues those whose spirits are crushed. (Psalm 34:18)

BETRAYAL

When Stephanie, our three kids, and I moved from small town Arkansas to South Florida more than twenty years ago, the bright lights of Miami and the legendary spring break stories of Fort Lauderdale beaches intimidated us, overwhelmed us, and made us feel lonely and small. We began our prayers every night by asking God for friends—people to do life with, to talk, laugh, and spend time together.

God answered our prayers after only a few weeks and brought two couples into our lives who were more than we could have imagined. They encouraged us when we struggled, supported us when we dreamed, and most importantly, they were always present! We worked together. We spent Christmas and summer vacations together. We even watched the Marlins win the World Series together. They made South Florida feel like home. They were, without a doubt, the best friends I have ever had.

But life is not static; it is always moving forward, at times slowly...and at times with incredible velocity. In the face of tensions between our friendship with one couple and my responsibilities to God and the church, I had to make a decision to do what I sincerely believed was the right thing: I had to choose God and the church. It was one of those disagreements that you try to work through, but in the end, it led to their sudden departure. Then a few years later, the other family unexpectedly decided to leave the area. I have never experienced a greater sense of loss than I did with the news of these departures. I prayed for friends, and God gave us friends. I felt as if I had failed because I did not maintain the friendship.

GOD IS ALWAYS WAITING

Once a close relationship ends, the most tragic thing you can do is hide and close yourself off from other people in a misguided effort to protect yourself from the pain of possible future heartaches. But God has not left your side. He is just waiting for you to respond to His call to realize your potential for greatness.

When these friendships came to an end, I remembered a lesson from King David:

He lifted me out of the pit of despair, out of the mud and the mire. He set my feet on solid ground and steadied me as I walked along. He has given me a new song to sing, a hymn of praise to our God. Many will see what he has done and be amazed. (Psalm 40:2–3)

These departures had left a vacancy in the church team, but in this case, God prepared and called Stephanie to step into her potential. Because she had not grown up in church ministry, Steph was hesitant to lead and had ceded her position to people who had more experience. However, this vacancy and our need for effective, bold leadership was just the impetus that Steph needed to reach her potential as a pastor, to speak and shepherd with confidence in ways she hadn't done before.

Even today, on days when the ministry feels lonely, I wonder if I made the right decision. However, I know that what I did was right for the church and for my friends. Their absence has also strengthened other friendships we had not previously had time to nurture and grow. This unexpected change has since filled our lives with companionship and joy once more.

When you look in the mirror, what do you see? I had to toss the Hawaiian shirts, tailored suits, and cigars on the floor to face who I intrinsically was: Troy Gramling. It's time for you to shed anything that is not *you* and do the same.

QUESTIONS FOR REFLECTION

We often wish we could be better than we are. But what is already *in your hand?* What are you good at? What are you passionate about?

Have you ever tried to emulate someone else instead of being your authentic self? What happened and what did you learn?

We all feel emotional pain at times. Who can you reach out to the next time you feel low instead of numbing yourself or avoiding the problem?

Do you know anyone who is going through a painful time? How can you reach out to help them?

Can you think of a time when you did the *right thing* even though it was the harder thing?

3

THE POWER OF SELF-AWARENESS: FROM INSECURITY TO STRENGTH

We all have character flaws we could work on—
and the key to improving them is simply paying attention.

Although I live in Florida, theme park capital of the world, I'm as bummed as any out-of-state visitor when I see signs on attractions that read, "Area being refurbished for your future enjoyment." Despite my disappointment, however, I understand that the ride is under repair, unfinished, or in need of improvements.

As people, we are much the same way. Regardless of our level of success, influence, or status, each of us is under refurbishment. We all lack something that will take us to the next level. The key is realizing what is needed—whether it's a new routine or a radical shift in thinking—and confronting the issue without fear of looking bad or weak.

If we don't look insecurity in the eye, it doesn't take long to become blind to it. The truly insecure go a step further. They start seeing their insecurities as the norm, as if everyone else has the problem, not them. Suppose there's a crooked painting on your living room wall. Do you adjust the frame…or blame the builders for the ceiling or floor being uneven because that's easier?

Do any of these phrases sound familiar?

+ "Dad was always angry, so I'm angry."

+ "I deserve to eat this junk food because I'm so stressed out!"

+ "My wife doesn't pay attention to me, so of course it's okay to watch this porn."

Insecure people live in a place that doesn't challenge them and excuses their idiosyncrasies. It's Denial 101, and if we're not careful, we can find ourselves there permanently.

Perhaps, like me, you have experienced God revealing to you through others what you have tried to hide privately. Have you changed the subject when a friend has pointed out one of your glaring character flaws? Do you interrupt people mid-sentence? Have you been annoyed by a family member's persistent habit, and then realized that you do the same annoying thing?

Although you may want to ignore the problem, hoping it goes away, realizing your weaknesses and mistakes is crucial to succeeding in life. If you are going to reach your potential, you must cast a naked eye upon yourself. When all is revealed to you and the world, healing can begin, and you can start to move forward.

We were born to win. To thrive. To figure out who we really are and leverage every opportunity to grow into the person God created us to be. So how do we do that? How do we become more self-aware and less insecure? It's not as hard as you may think.

LET'S GET REAL ABOUT MOSES

The reason I love the story of Moses goes beyond the drama of his birth, his courage in leading the Israelites out of slavery, or how God used him to part the Red Sea. I love the fact that he was so *human*. He was weak. He looked for excuses. He screwed up.

If there was hope for Moses, there is hope for us!

Even after God appeared to Moses in a burning bush, calling him to lead His chosen people out of slavery, then performed two amazing wonders to demonstrate the power He would provide through his hands, Moses still doubted that he was the man for the job!

> *But Moses pleaded with the* LORD, *"O Lord, I'm not very good with words. I never have been, and I'm not now, even though you have spoken to me. I get tongue-tied, and my words get tangled."*
>
> (Exodus 4:10)

Moses can't answer God's call because he's not a good speaker? He even tells God, *"Lord, please! Send anyone else"* (Exodus 4:13). It's safe to say that God is frustrated with Moses at this point. Of course, God is aware that Moses is flawed, as much as any human. But what Moses doesn't appreciate at this point—and what you may not realize either—is that he will not have to do this job alone. He has the power of God at his fingertips. And so do you!

Angry with Moses, God instructs him to enlist his brother Aaron to speak for him, take his shepherd's staff, and get going! In a similar way, in this chapter, if you can become more self-aware, you can fortify yourself with what you need to succeed.

Winning at life demands that we be keenly aware of who we are as husbands, mothers, students, employees, leaders, and Christ followers. It's replacing the telescope through which we normally view ourselves with a big old magnifying glass. We need to really zero in on what we see (and what everyone else sees) with deliberate and intentional honesty.

> *WHAT IS NECESSARY TO CHANGE A PERSON IS TO*
> *CHANGE HIS AWARENESS OF HIMSELF.*
> —ABRAHAM MASLOW

No time like the present to remedy our *lack* of self-awareness. Over the past couple of decades, I have worked on myself and helped my staff, my congregation, and my family to increase self-awareness using four steps that begin with the letter L—*list, look, listen,* and *learn.*

1. LIST YOUR INSECURITIES

When you list your insecurities, they'll lose some of their power over you.

One Wednesday night during a leadership meeting, I asked the group to complete a simple assignment: *Write down your top three insecurities.*

I could just feel the tension in the room.

But I invite you right now to do the same. Maybe use the margin of this page or a separate notebook. List the three things about yourself that cause you the greatest stress. (If you need to write it in code, feel free.) Don't worry! Nobody will see this but you, unless you've written it on this page and lend the book to someone else.

What are my three greatest insecurities? The first and most stressful is what I'm doing at this very moment: writing something that someone else will read. While I believe I have something to say, I'm not very confident in how I'm saying it. This dates back to something that happened in fourth grade. (More on that in chapter seven.) Even if it's just a tweet or an Instagram post, I get nervous. Are my spelling and grammar correct? Am I making sense? Did I get my point across?

My second insecurity is social events. As I mentioned earlier, I'm a bit of an introvert, so when it comes to casual conversations, I'm not sure I have anything interesting to add. I'd rather people-watch from the corner any day than work the room.

And third, with the passing of another year, I become stressed about whether there is enough time to accomplish all of the things I dreamed of doing!

NOW SHARE YOUR LIST!

Do you have your three? Let's make it a little tougher. *Share those three insecurities with someone else.*

I asked the leaders at that meeting to turn to their neighbor and trade answers. I'm not cruel, I assure you! It was for their own good. Many squirmed, just like you may be doing right now. It isn't easy. Far from it. Realizing our weak spots is hard enough, but telling someone else? Unheard of. Barbaric. But necessary.

If you don't have a list, maybe one of your insecurities is admitting that you have them! That's okay. But if you want to win at life, you need to realize that none of us has it all together. *You* could use some refining, just like everyone else.

2. LOOK AT OTHER PEOPLE'S CONDUCT

Look at other people's conduct and behavior. How does yours compare?

As I mentioned, here in South Florida, we are just a few hours away from Walt Disney World and Universal Studios in Orlando. We visit these theme parks fairly often, but while my kids and grandkids ride the roller coasters and my wife shops, I just park myself on a bench somewhere to people-watch. How do they interact with one another? What is that guy's body language saying to his wife? How are that brother and sister handling apparent conflict? In my head, I make mental notes—not just of their behaviors, but also how my behavior with others may be the same or different.

I am a student of human behavior and conduct. Why? Because if I understand the thought processes and tendencies of others, I can better understand how I appear when I am facing similar situations. If a guy in a store has a fight with the clerk and uses words that are less than kind, now I know what it will sound like if I say them. It's the same reason I like to watch local government meetings on TV. (Yes, I know what you're thinking. I'm *that guy*. Someone has to watch those meetings, right?) I like to see the mayor interact with the concerned citizens, or watch disgruntled business owners spar with their elected council representative. I learn from their behavior. I put myself in their place. And when I do, I have a much better snapshot of what it would look like when or if I made those same choices.

Observing others and their reactions helps me decide if I want to react the same way, should the same situation arise in my own life. It's scenario-based self-awareness training. By taking the time to study the actions of others, I get a better idea on how people respond to me now, and what I could become if I act in similar ways in the future.

3. LISTEN TO THOSE AROUND YOU

Do you listen—truly, sincerely listen—to the people around you?

It's easy to spot the listeners among the people we know because they are constantly surrounded by other people. There are far more talkers, fixers, problem-solvers, and critics than there are listeners.

Listeners are people with an open and nonjudgmental ear who offer themselves as sounding boards and confidantes. Skilled in the art of head-nodding and engagement, they are quick to offer a smile over a solution. Listening is a key skill in the journey toward self-awareness, and one that may come easier to some than others.

When I was the pastor of a church in Arkansas, I spent a lot of time setting up special weekends that I was sure would draw crowds. I would promote the upcoming sermon topic on the church sign (we didn't have social media back then), spend hours on my sermon, and tell everyone I knew that they just *had* to be there this weekend. It was going to be a sermon that would change their lives forever. Then Sunday would come, and I would triumphantly throw open the front doors...only to find the same few people who came every week. I was crestfallen. So I did what many do. I took it out on those who were there.

PREACHING TO THE CHOIR

I'd stand in the pulpit and pound my hand down on the hard wood, yelling, "This city needs Jesus! I wish this community understood what the word *loyalty* meant. Then they'd be here every weekend!" When I finished my rant, I would sulk to the back of the church to shake hands with those who were in attendance.

One weekend, a sweet older member approached me and said, "Pastor, no disrespect intended, but why are you yelling at us? *We're the ones who are here!*" Then it hit me. I was talking and not listening. I was literally preaching to the choir—hurting those who already agreed with me. I had completely forgotten that in life, sometimes the people who hear us the loudest are often not the people we feel the need to reach.

Many people have no idea who they are or how they appear to others because they simply don't leave space in a conversation to find out. They are so busy defending themselves that they miss what they were supposed to hear. The key to becoming less insecure and more self-aware is to simply open your ears and close your mouth as much as possible. Scripture puts it this way:

> *Understand this, my dear brothers and sisters: You must all be quick to listen, slow to speak, and slow to get angry.*   (James 1:19)

Are you *quick to listen?* Ask yourself these questions:

+ Do you listen to really learn from and understand the other person, or are you just being polite?

+ Are you more intent on getting your points across rather than letting the conversation take its own direction?

+ Do you ask questions?

+ Is your ratio of talking and listening fairly even?

+ Do you repeat what you have heard to ensure that you understand it?

+ Do you wait until the other person is done speaking before you respond?

Self-awareness is rooted in self-control and being aware of who's listening to who. Understand when to share your opinion and when to bite your tongue. Want to know if you are a good listener? Ask someone you are close to. Be willing to accept their feedback and grow from it. We all may think we're good listeners but look around you. If you're standing alone, it might be because you aren't aware of how one-sided your conversations tend to be.

4. LEARN FROM OTHERS

A fourth way to become more self-aware and less insecure is to ask loved ones and people you trust how they think others perceive you. Ask questions. What adjectives would they use to describe your temperament? Do others see you the way you see yourself?

These are extremely hard questions for anyone to ask, but the road to self-awareness is paved with deliberate and eye-opening realizations about ourselves.

A word of caution, however. We can't ask just anyone. Everybody has an opinion. The server who brought you your lunch might think you're a generous tipper. Your third-grade teacher may remember you as the quiet kid who liked to color every page with the same crayon. Your mom and dad see their younger selves. Your girlfriend or boyfriend sees you romantically. The critic sees you as someone they disagree with. The overachiever can often see you as someone in their way to the top. Everybody's lens is different. And all of them want to speak into your life in some way.

So who do you listen to? Whose opinion do you let in? Stick to these three categories:

1. People who love you. Those who truly love you, not what you can do for them or give them, should be able to give you an honest opinion.

2. People who believe in you. They may not love you or even like you, but if they see your greatness and potential, they will want to help you succeed.

3. People who know more than you do. If their knowledge in your field exceeds yours, you should give their opinion more weight. This type of person will make you aware of what you don't know and help fill in the gaps. This will help your confidence grow and your insecurities diminish.

If an opinion comes from anyone outside these three categories, I'll listen to it, but I don't hold it as close to my heart. At one time, we could count on reading or hearing informed opinions from people who had risen through the ranks and gained respect. But in this digital age, with social media and Yelp, *everyone* has an opinion. I want to know how the world sees me—but if I give equal weight to the opinions of outsiders and people who are close to me, I will spend every day feeling increasingly insecure and get nowhere.

The path to self-awareness is not for the faint of heart or little faith. But if you're willing to reach out and risk a little embarrassment, you can reemerge more self-aware and secure in *who you are, where you are going,* and *what you have been gifted to do.*

In my early years of pastoring, I was driven to reach my potential but insecure about how to do it. I would often reach out to people who loved me, believed in me, or knew more about ministry than me to ask for their feedback—and then nervously await their response.

What I discovered is that the attitude that led me to honestly ask the question about how I was perceived led to more growth than I could have ever expected!

CONFIDENCE IS DECIDING YOU'RE UNSTOPPABLE—
NOT THAT YOU'LL NEVER FAIL.
—TOM BILYEU

RESPECT THE QUEST

Have you ever had a Quest Protein Bar? You might be surprised to learn that the cofounder of Quest Nutrition, Tom Bilyeu, grew up in Tacoma, Washington, in a poor family that struggled with obesity. He says he was a lazy, chubby child. Bilyeu didn't believe he would go far in life—and says that his mother didn't either! On his first job delivering papers, he was too shy to collect his paycheck. Bilyeu says he cheated his way through high school and only attended the University of Southern California because his mother made him. But in college, he decided to pursue a film career, became obsessed with health and fitness, and lost sixty pounds.

While in college, Bilyeu began to work for a tech company called Awareness Tech. He had two goals: work his way up the ranks and make money. And after several years, he achieved them both. But he found himself unfulfilled. He tried to quit, but his partners wouldn't let him—they wanted to remain partners in whatever Bilyeu had planned next!

Bilyeu decided that his next company would focus on creating *value*, not money. In 2010, Bilyeu, his wife, and three other partners cofounded Quest Nutrition on the premise that "food can be good for you and still taste good." Its mission was to end the litany of health conditions—heart disease, stroke, and type 2 diabetes—that contribute to metabolic syndrome, which Bilyeu believed was at an epidemic level throughout the world. The Mayo Clinic says that up to one-third of US adults suffer from it.[3] Bilyeu and his partners started making healthy nutrition bars out of their kitchen before Awareness Tech was even sold. They perfected a recipe with no added sugar, but were turned down by every manufacturer. That didn't stop them; they built the equipment themselves and continued to make their products. Before long, Quest exploded.

By 2014, *Inc.* magazine called Quest the second fastest growing company in North America. Bilyeu and partners sold the company to Simply Good Foods Co. in 2019—nine years after founding it—for $1 billion!

Tom Bilyeu had actually stepped down from Quest Nutrition a few years before this to turn his attention to what he saw as a second worldwide epidemic: "The poverty of poor mindset." He explains, "Just because you start weak doesn't mean you have to stay weak."[4] His media company, Impact Theory, is focused solely on creating content that empowers people. His YouTube channel has nearly 4 million subscribers around the world.

Insecurity is indeed at epidemic levels. It hobbled Moses in his lifetime, but once he realized he was *not alone*, that God would be right beside him, he took the next step toward his potential. And you will too.

Open your heart, give voice to your insecurities, and share them. Open your eyes to how others behave. Open your ears to the feedback of trusted loved ones. When you take these steps, you will open yourself up to your limitless potential, the uncontainable power of God within you.

---

3. "Metabolic syndrome," Mayo Clinic, May 6, 2021, www.mayoclinic.org/diseases-conditions/metabolic-syndrome/symptoms-causes/syc-20351916.
4. Gerard Adams, "The Simple Way to Find Your Passion, According to a Founder Who Built a Billion-Dollar Brand," *Inc.*, January 31, 2018, www.inc.com/gerard-adams/the-simple-way-to-find-your-passion-according-to-a-founder-who-built-a-billion-dollar-brand.html.

IF YOU LOOK FOR THE NEGATIVE,
IT WILL BE THERE. IF YOU LOOK FOR THE POSITIVE,
IT WILL OVERWHELM YOU.
—TOM BILYEU

QUESTIONS FOR REFLECTION

When has God used others to reveal to you something that you have tried to hide privately?

Make a list of your top three insecurities. (Remember, mine are writing, social events, and not accomplishing everything I'd like to in this life.) Can you think of someone you could share these with? How would it feel?

Can you think of a time you've observed someone's good behavior or deeds? How can you model that in your life?

Are you a good listener? Do you absorb what someone is saying to you and ask questions? Do you let the other person talk, or do you do most of the talking?

List three people whose opinions you respect—someone who loves you; someone who believes in you; and someone who knows more than you do. Make a point of including these people in your future decisions.

4

THE POWER OF VOICE: PROCLAIMING THE VISION

Time to give voice to the potential that God has whispered to you, and you've finally chosen to hear.

Reflecting back to 1990, when I stood in the kitchen of our tiny apartment and shared with Stephanie my *nudge* toward ministry, I wish that I could have a re-do. I imagine pushing a rewind button on the giant screen of my life so I could approach that conversation differently. Several things I said and the way I said them would be better now. However, since rewind buttons for life are not an option at present, I've resolved to accept that youthful error and now hope to share some important truths with you.

Looking back, I realize that I did not share my vision with confidence. *I had not set myself up for success.*

- *I didn't pick the right time or place.* Rather than having the conversation on a relaxing Sunday afternoon over a late lunch, after we had enjoyed teaching the youth class, I chose a weeknight when we were going in a million directions. We were both working, finishing up college, and had a paper route for which we set our alarms at 3 a.m. every weekday morning. By 10 p.m., we were both exhausted. And rather than sharing my *revelation* to Steph sitting comfortably in the living room, or even resting in bed, I chose to proclaim it standing in the kitchen.

- *I wasn't prepared.* I didn't think through how this pronouncement would impact literally *everything*. Steph and I had talked, dreamed, and planned for our life in education and coaching; her family members were all educators. What did this *call to ministry* mean? Would I still teach, or was this a whole new direction? Steph is a very detailed person; I knew that. And yet I had not prepared answers to the questions I knew she would have.

- *I wasn't clear.* I had spent months wrestling with, praying about, and even talking to others about this calling. But I didn't include Stephanie on that journey. So rather than sharing my excitement that I had come to a conclusion, she didn't even know I was having this internal conflict. A big mistake! Today, I would confide in Steph on day one—well, okay, by day three, for sure! But she would already know; she would see it on my face. We got married young. After thirty years of marriage, we are able to communicate without words. It doesn't mean we should, but we can.

After I made what we call *my big speech*, I learned a lot about marriage, communication, and leadership. And I learned something that had always been right in front of me:

Where there is no vision, the people perish.   (Proverbs 29:18 KJV)

"The people" in this case was Steph, and while she fortunately did not perish, she *did* get really confused and push back!

IN ORDER TO SERVE ITS PURPOSE,
A VISION HAS TO BE A SHARED VISION.
—WARREN G. BENNIS

BUT FIRST, BEGIN WITH A VISION

Before any careers are launched, before any buildings are built, before any businesses are started, and before any social media accounts are created, there must be a vision. You can't go someplace you can't envision.

One of the great benefits of being a Christ follower is that the vision begins with a word from God, what we call *wisdom*.

The *New Living Translation* of Proverbs 29:18 says, *"When people do not accept divine guidance, they run wild. But whoever obeys the law is joyful."*

VISION IS A PICTURE OF THE FUTURE THAT
PRODUCES PASSION.
—BILL HYBELS

Vision wakes you up in the morning and keeps you up at night. So I ask you, "What is the wisdom, dream, or vision God has placed in your heart that causes it to beat fast?"

For me, it was to devote my life to preaching the Word of God, to see people embrace the potential they were created to bring to life. How was I going to do that? I wasn't quite sure. But I trusted that divine guidance, that whisper. In my experience, God will show you what He's going to do, but He doesn't do it immediately.

Think of it as walking along a path before sunrise. It's a little hard to find your way, to know how wide it is, where the curves and boundaries are. But as the sun rises, the path becomes clearer. It's the same with a vision. But you have to take the first step! I trusted that if I headed in the right direction, the path would become clear.

FAITH IS TAKING THE FIRST STEP EVEN WHEN YOU DON'T SEE THE WHOLE STAIRCASE.
—DR. MARTIN LUTHER KING, JR.

So many people think they have to see the whole path before they take the first step toward their potential. And guess what? They never attain it. While I could very easily have taken a teaching and coaching job, it would have led in a different direction and taken my focus away from the vision that God implanted in me. Though the long-term vision was not clear, what *was* clear was my next step—to become the person He was calling me to be. So I studied, I prayed, I learned, and I leaned into Him. But that also looked like saying *no* to other plans, even ones that were the source of youthful dreams.

Clarifying the vision in your own heart and mind and then making difficult decisions based on that vision is just the beginning. You also need to cast the vision to others. One person is not enough to accomplish greatness.

Steph's love for God and me overcame my ill-conceived first attempt at casting vision for our future. Afterward, I vowed that the next time I cast a vision, I would listen to God first so that my timing, preparation, and clarity would be acted upon with confidence.

FEW PEOPLE ATTAIN GREAT LIVES,
IN LARGE PART BECAUSE IT IS JUST SO
EASY TO SETTLE FOR A GOOD LIFE.
—JIM COLLINS

DON'T SETTLE FOR "A GOOD LIFE"

I have read and reread Jim Collins's book *Good to Great: Why Some Companies Make the Leap and Others Don't* many times. His focus is on successful companies, but companies are run by people, and people are motivated by a vision.

Why do we settle for good when we are created for greatness? Why do we make compromises? Stay in jobs we don't like? Not try our best in school, on the playing field, or in our relationships?

Everyone always thinks of Moses as a strong, fearless leader, but he had his moments of doubt just like we do, times when he was flawed, hesitant, and afraid. The vision that God had promised—leading him and his people out of slavery to a promised land—was just so big! Wouldn't good be *good enough?*

I often think about the small community of Paragould where I grew up. It's a factory town with good, hard-working people. For many, working in a factory gives them the schedule and the income to do things that they enjoy. I've seen some people work third shift so that they can run their own farm during the day, play a sport, or go hunting.

Factories often pay well and offer great insurance plans; they can be secure places to work in insecure times. But for a few, working in a factory can feel like a life sentence. They start working when they are young, intending for it to be *just for now.* But time passes so quickly that *now* becomes yesterday, today, and tomorrow. These folks, who don't enjoy their work, regret that *just for now* has become several decades. Some of them made a deal and traded their future for a paycheck.

This book is for these folks too. By God's grace, there is time! He hasn't given up on you or His vision for you.

You have a vision. You have thought about it for years. Maybe it's time to share it with someone. Maybe today is the day you take a step in the direction of the promised land.

+ Register for college.

+ Fill out a particular job application.

+ Ask someone to mentor you.

The sacrifice will be high and the challenge will be great, but you will not regret it.

VISION WITHOUT ACTION IS JUST A DREAM, ACTION WITHOUT VISION JUST PASSES THE TIME, AND VISION WITH ACTION CAN CHANGE THE WORLD.
—NELSON MANDELA

THIS ISN'T A GAME SHOW: NO DEALS

In May 2003, I had just been named lead pastor at Potential Church. Thirteen years had passed since that conversation in the kitchen. I would be succeeding Pastor Dan Southerland, the most popular and respected pastor in the twenty-year history of the church, who led it to grow from 300 to more than 2,000 congregants. I should have been intimidated, maybe even afraid! But I had not forgotten what I learned about timing, preparation, and clarity. I spent weeks meeting and talking with the volunteer leaders, the staff, and the congregation. They had just started their largest building project to date before I came, and they needed to raise the money to fund it. So the timing for something new was perfect.

God had been preparing me for this moment through the previous church that Steph and I had planted and the multiple building projects we had completed there. I had shared the vision with the board, the staff, and the volunteer leaders, so by the time I was going to share it with the congregation, it had been refined multiple times for clarity.

Here was my vision:

+ Instead of being another church on a corner, we would have *50 campuses and church plants*, including those in places people don't normally go to start campuses and plant churches.

+ We would be a church of *100,000 people* from different parts of the country, with different racial backgrounds. Men and women, young and old, gathered together with unified purpose to carry out the commandment to love the Lord our God with all our heart, soul, and mind, and love our neighbors as ourselves. In other words, we were going to partner with people to reach their God-given potential in order to impact the world for good.

+ We would go around the world with *$150 million* to help the hurting, feed the hungry, and most importantly to share the gospel.

It was my *50-100-150 plan*.

Prepared as I was, I hesitated before my presentation to the congregation. Wasn't this vision a little *too* visionary? The debate I had with myself before proclaiming my vision for Potential Church aloud sounds a lot like the negotiation between Moses and Pharaoh before Moses led the Israelites out of Egypt.

Let's remember where Moses is at this time. God has sent awful judgment upon Pharaoh and his people in the form of ten devastating plagues.

And Pharaoh offered to let God's people go—but he wanted them to go on his terms. Four times, he offered to let them leave, but each time, he attached a condition and a compromise to their leaving. He wanted Moses and Israel to trade what God had promised them—that they would be set free from slavery and be delivered to the promised land—for something less.

That inner struggle between belief and doubt, action and inaction, and faith and fear are deeply human experiences. I wrestled with myself before I shared my vision with anyone. I remember the temptation from the very beginning to concede. I thought to myself: 50-100-150 is crazy! Nobody is going to believe you. Just be quiet. Yet I was compelled to follow Moses's lead and say, "No deal." And you are going to do that too.

I once heard a sermon by Pastor Rod Parsley entitled "Let's Make a Deal," and it made me think of the old TV show, *Let's Make a Deal*. The original show debuted in December 1963, and various episodes still air in the US and many countries around the world. The audience dressed in crazy, outrageous costumes, each trying to get the attention of the host, Monty Hall, so they could run up, arms waving, and be a contestant or *trader*. Hall would offer them something of value, which they could keep or exchange for something else. But *that* item was hidden in a box or behind a curtain. So the trader might be getting a better prize...or a *zonk*, something worthless, a dud.

What does the game show *Let's Make a Deal* have to do with Moses, my plan for Potential Church, or whatever your vision might be, whether it's a new career, a new business, or starting a family?

It's about the word *concession*. *Merriam-Webster's Dictionary* defines *concession* as "something done or agreed to usually grudgingly in order to reach an agreement or improve a situation."

To concede "to reach an agreement or improve a situation"? While that may be true in a court of law, it is definitely *not* true on the basketball court or in any athletic contest. When I hear the word *concede*, I hear, "give up ground" and "surrender." I can still hear my college coach today, yelling from the bench, "Troy, don't concede the lane!"

The *lane* is that different-colored space on the basketball court closest to the basket. My coach was telling me not to give up ground, especially ground that was important to the outcome of the game. (A coach today might yell, "Don't concede the three-point line!" but it's the same message.) Don't settle for something that will eventually lead to your defeat!

Pharaoh wanted Moses to concede on God's plan—to either give up entirely or make compromises, just as you and I are tempted to do before sharing our vision. But there are no upgrades when we do so, only *zonks*. The voice of doubt will offer you every compromise at its disposal to attempt to lead you astray.

Let's look at the four *deals* Pharaoh had for Moses:

DEAL #1: DON'T GO

In Exodus 5:1, Moses is finally ready to speak the vision to Pharaoh:

After this presentation to Israel's leaders, Moses and Aaron went and spoke to Pharaoh. They told him, "This is what the LORD, the God of Israel, says: 'Let my people go so they may hold a festival in my honor in the wilderness.'"

But even after some plagues, Pharaoh says, in effect, "Let's make a deal, Moses! You can serve your God, but you don't have to leave Egypt to do it. Do it here." (See Exodus 8:25.)

Pharaoh is suspicious that this is a ploy on behalf of the Israelites to flee Egypt. Why does the festival need to be held in the wilderness? Why does it matter? They are fine where they are. Does that deal sound familiar? You may have heard something along these lines:

+ *Go ahead and be a Christian if you want to, but don't change your lifestyle!*

+ *You can be saved and still be just like everyone else.*

+ *Don't go. You can pursue your dream and stay where you are.*

The enemy has tried this deal in my life on numerous occasions! I remember the offer that kept playing over and over in my mind: You can be a pastor *and* a coach. There is no doubt that this is exactly what some are called to do. But I knew that for me to pick up a basketball and a whistle was to concede to the enemy.

The same thing happened at Potential Church before I shared my 50-100-150 plan. The deal that I continued to wrestle with was, "Pastor, don't push." Lead, but stay here. Multiple campuses and church plants are complex and difficult. Are they even possible?

The first concession would be to quit or settle for things as they are. Why make your life harder?

DEAL #2: DON'T DREAM

In Exodus 8:28, Pharaoh says that Moses and the Israelites can go— but not very far:

"All right, go ahead," Pharaoh replied. "I will let you go into the wilderness to offer sacrifices to the LORD your God. But don't go too far away. Now hurry and pray for me."

It's funny, when we are ordering french fries and soda, we supersize, but when it comes to our dreams, we downsize. Why is that? I remember struggling with myself before I shared my dream for Potential Church. I thought to myself, "Do you have to give actual numbers, 50-100-150? They're so set in stone! Just talk about growing the church or reaching people, and that's enough!" But a vision downsized is not a vision at all.

It's human to feel inadequate or unprepared, but we are talking about the divine wisdom and potential within us.

God has a plan for you; He has shared it to you in a whisper. But you must be true to it. Don't make any deals that diminish it!

DEAL #3: DON'T TELL EVERYONE

Accountability is a powerful word. What some would call the fear of failure, I would call the fear of being culpable if things don't go as planned. It can keep us from even *imagining* what the future could be.

After being threatened with a plague of locusts, Pharaoh attempts to get Moses to just take the adult men to worship in the wilderness, leaving the women and children behind. He tells Moses:

> *"The Lord will certainly need to be with you if I let you take your little ones! I can see through your evil plan. Never! Only the men may go and worship the Lord, since that is what you requested." And Pharaoh threw them out of the palace.* (Exodus 10:10–11)

Pharaoh knows if they don't take everybody, they will be back. And Moses may have thought, "Well, is *everyone's* participation required? Maybe we can leave the women and children here. Is that concession breaking the covenant of Abraham?"

The answer is yes.

When Steph and I moved from Arkansas to Florida, we intentionally made decisions that would make backtracking difficult. First, we purchased our house in Florida, knowing that if it didn't work out, it would be hard to move back. Second, we intentionally did *not* call Arkansas *home.* We wanted the kids to look at *Florida* as home, not Arkansas. It didn't make our family in Arkansas happy, but it committed us to the vision.

If we just tell a few people about our vision, we can always levy an excuse or even downsize our dream. But once others start talking about our vision, it's out there. It's amazing how easily people forget so many of the things we say—but they seem to always remember what we tell them we are going to do.

You can tell a child to clean his room a hundred times, and he will swear that he *forgot*. But mention just once that you are going to do something—particularly something they *want* you to do—and they will not only remember it but they will also remind you of what you said. That's selective hearing!

DEAL #4: DON'T COMMIT

Have you heard some people *talk* about their vision but watched them hold back on executing it until they see how everyone is going to respond?

In Exodus 10:24, Pharaoh ultimately agrees to let Moses and all of the Israelite men, women, and children go...but they must leave all of their resources in Egypt:

Finally, Pharaoh called for Moses. "Go and worship the LORD," he said. "But leave your flocks and herds here. You may even take your little ones with you."

But God had said to Moses:

I will be with you. And this is your sign that I am the one who has sent you: When you have brought the people out of Egypt, you will worship God at this very mountain. (Exodus 3:12)

The Lord was not clear about what would be required for the sacrifices and feasting, but the people would have to be prepared with *everything they had* when the moment came.

Pharaoh was offering for them to go but leave their resources behind. However, because Moses didn't take the deal, when the Israelites left to worship God and pursue the land He had promised them, they were enriched by the Egyptians who had enslaved them!

And the people of Israel did as Moses had instructed; they asked the Egyptians for clothing and articles of silver and gold. The LORD caused *the Egyptians to look favorably on the Israelites, and they gave the Israelites whatever they asked for. So **they stripped the Egyptians of their wealth!*** (Exodus 12:35–36)

In order to build a church or start a business, you often need a loan from the bank. When you are in the early days of your endeavor, the bank will ask for what they call a personal guarantee in order to make the loan. In other words, they want you to put your name on the dotted line to say that even if the church or business can't pay back what you've borrowed, you will guarantee repayment.

While Steph and I never hesitated to put our names on that dotted line, I have been amazed at the number of church pastors who won't. They are willing to go for the dream, but don't you dare ask them to risk *their* resources on it.

We didn't need our name on the loan papers for my 50-100-150 plan, but the dream of multiple campuses required an executive team that was completely committed to the idea.

The entire team took pay cuts in order to hire the individuals we needed to see the vision come alive.

My experience is that those who take a deal never arrive in the land God has promised. A vision starts with a whisper—but if it is never given full voice, it will fail. God shared the vision with Moses. Then Moses shared it with Aaron. Moses and Aaron went to Egypt to share the vision with the Israelites. And finally, they shared the vision with Pharaoh: "Let my people go!"

Leaders are made for community. You aren't meant to carry the vision by yourself.

A LONG JOURNEY

The whisper that I shared with Stephanie more than twenty years ago—my calling to become a pastor—became our shared vision. It took us to Potential Church, and our goal for fifty campuses and church plants, a congregation of 100,000, and $150 million to help the hurting, feed the hungry, and share the gospel around the world. We have been on that journey for the last twenty- plus years.

It has taken longer, cost more, and been more difficult than I would have ever believed. We have opened campuses, and we have closed some. We have planted churches, and we have also had to give up some. We have had weekends with more than 30,000 people in attendance, and as a result of COVID-19, we had weekends where the police showed up to make sure there were no more than ten people there.

We will talk about how to deal with the different challenges to your vision from other people and outside circumstances in later chapters. But the biggest obstacle to your vision being accomplished comes from the same person who was trying to get you to make a deal before you ever proclaimed your vision—you!

NO DEALS! DO OR DIE!

In 1519, Spanish conquistador Hernán Cortés arrived in Mexico with six hundred men after a long and dangerous journey. He reportedly sank his ships as his troops prepared for the impossible feat ahead: the battle, defeat, and plunder of the Aztec Empire.

Be accountable for your vision. Do or die! Sink or swim! No deal!

Like Moses and Cortés, we must refuse to diminish our visions. Until we commit to the vision with our heart, words, and actions, it will remain out of reach.

We are tempted by deals because they look possible. We start to believe we can accomplish our dreams and not have to sacrifice, reach our potential and not have to commit, and live out our purpose without being accountable.

But these are all lies, cooked up by the father of lies. They come from the same place as the deals that Pharaoh tried to make with Moses. The devil is an enemy to your potential, to your calling, to your dreams. But these are deals you don't have to make. It is ground you must not *concede* if you are going to *succeed*!

Let's Make a Deal episodes played in my mind before I shared my 50-100-150 vision publicly. Part of me said, "Wait! Don't do anything drastic! Don't make any sacrifices!"

But I had already begun putting steps into place that would allow us to move forward. It had begun thirteen years earlier in a small kitchen in Paragould, Arkansas, and it had led us to a moment when we took $10,000 out of our retirement accounts to make our vision of 50-100-150 a reality. More on that later. For now, it's enough to remind you to shout from the rooftops what God has whispered in your heart!

ACTUALLY, I'M AN OVERNIGHT SUCCESS.
BUT IT TOOK TWENTY YEARS.
—MONTY HALL

QUESTIONS FOR REFLECTION

Can you think of a time when you shared your vision prematurely? When you weren't clear, hadn't done your homework, or picked the wrong time? How could you have reframed the situation?

What is the wisdom, dream, or vision God has placed in your heart that causes it to beat fast?

What are three things you can do right now to advance yourself toward that vision?

STEP TWO:
CHALLENGES

5

THE POWER OF DISRUPTION: THE ROUNDABOUT WAY

God took the Israelites on a long and winding road toward success. We're going that way, too.

The roundabout way is a concept I have studied and sometimes wrestled with over the years. In fact, the story of Moses and the Israelites' circuitous journey to the promised land was the subject of the first sermon I preached as lead pastor at Potential Church in 2003. I started in the main auditorium and then went backstage as Pastor Dan had often done, but then I pretended to not know how to get to the stage. I would pop my head out of different doors or end up in the baptistry, anywhere and everywhere other than where I needed to be.

Many of those in the congregation only saw me as the guy in the parking lot. They had no idea why I was on staff at Potential Church, or the years of experience I had brought with me. Just as it appeared to take a bit longer than expected to find my way to the stage, God had also taken me on what I call the roundabout way to get to Potential. Along the way, I'd had some doubts, been discouraged, and even made some wrong decisions. But I got there!

I learned—as the Israelites did and as you will too—that the roundabout way is not meant to be a time of *punishment* but rather *preparation*.

When the Israelites started on their journey to the promised land, they had been liberated from generations of slavery in Egypt. They were free people with money and some really nice clothes, which God had promised them, and the Egyptians gave them. However, instead of guiding them to enter the promised land from the south, a journey that would have taken eleven days, God led them east. He took them the roundabout way to prepare them for their future, but their bad decisions added forty years to their journey!

ARE WE THERE YET?

Now I know good things come to those who wait, haste makes waste, patience is a virtue, and all of those other true but trite sayings as well as anyone. But Moses had already lived in the desert for forty years. He was eighty years old! The Israelites had lived their entire lives as slaves. After being freed, they had a new lease on life.

As a leader myself, I used to wonder, "Does it have to be this hard?" When I first began to think about the story of Moses, I was confused. Why was the roundabout way, the longer route, the better way?

When you're young, you have very little to lose. You're ready to take on any challenge and yet God takes you the *longer way*, often in a direction that seems like the wrong direction. We live in a culture that celebrates and markets to the young, but maybe God values maturity and perseverance that can only be obtained through experience. Guess what? Experience takes time. The roundabout way may not be the preferred route but, in the end, it is the necessary route if you truly want to succeed!

I came to understand that if the Israelites had taken the quickest route, they would have had to overcome incredible obstacles for which God knew they were not ready. They might have become so discouraged that they returned to Egypt. So God sent them on the roundabout way, which took longer but gave them small victories during their journey. Their faith in God and their confidence both grew.

TO THRIVE ONCE YOU ARRIVE

Success is more than just arriving at a destination; it's enjoying yourself once you get there. For example, Hollywood is filled with very public examples of people who arrive at a destination called *success* at a very young age, only to be incredibly unhappy later. The roundabout way gives us the skills necessary to not only arrive, but to thrive.

I often think about the actual landscape the Israelites were traveling in the Red Sea region. The fact that it wasn't a jungle or forest type of wilderness, where they couldn't see what was in front of them, made it worse. It was a scrubby, dusty desert; they could see for miles, but they saw nothing! As far as they walked, it was difficult to see progress. The promised land seemed just as far away as it had the day before.

As hard as it is for you to acknowledge your potential, give voice to your calling, and then take the first step toward it, nothing is more difficult than the wilderness that inevitably follows. At the beginning of the journey, you've defeated the adversary, which is often just your lack of self-confidence. You're checking off boxes on the way to your goal, be it finishing your resume, launching your website, selling your first pizza, or eating a healthier diet. You've got some early wins.

Then you start hitting detours, dead ends, or dry holes. Maybe you write a book that several publishers reject. Orders slow down. You've sent out ten job applications and haven't heard anything. Your likes on Facebook dwindle. The doctor says getting pregnant could take months. The desert path feels long and endless.

GETTING TIRED OF "MANNA"

After ten years at Potential Church, I had that feeling of discouragement. I was checking off the boxes. In fact, I had been checking them off my whole life—game points, wins, graduation, marriage, children, job, ministry, assistant pastor, lead pastor. Progress, rewards, wins. In my first few years at Potential, it more than doubled in size. We added staff, enlarged the school, started five Potential church campuses, and partnered with multiple church planters. We fed thousands of hungry people, saw marriages restored, and witnessed lives changed. But when you're somewhere as long as I've been now, people get tired of the manna.

As the Israelites wandered in the desert, they began to complain about the manna. Remember, God had given them a plentiful food source. No one was going to starve. But after a while, the Israelites got tired of it and started to whine:

"Oh, for some meat!" they exclaimed. "We remember the fish we used to eat for free in Egypt. And we had all the cucumbers, melons, leeks, onions, and garlic we wanted. But now our appetites are gone. All we ever see is this manna!" (Numbers 11:4–6)

So for a month, God sent them flocks of quail to eat—so much meat that they grew sick of it. (See Numbers 11:20.) Later, they continued to complain about the manna:

Why have you brought us out of Egypt to die here in the wilderness?... There is nothing to eat here and nothing to drink. And we hate this horrible manna! (Numbers 21:5)

Wow, they certainly had short memories! They'd been *slaves* back in Egypt. Did they not remember they had been freed from slavery? That they were God's chosen ones, on the way to the land of milk and honey? They were comparing manna to what they previously had instead of what they could have, which was a much greater reward! In other words, they were filled with doubt.

When in the wilderness, the question is always one of arrival: *Are we ever going to get there?*

But if you're in the wilderness on the roundabout way, you are right where you are supposed to be.

What we see from the weeds is not what God sees from above. Read that again. God leads according to the *needs* of our heart, not its *desires*. By taking the Israelites on the roundabout way, He was trying to teach them perseverance, patience, fortitude, and maturity.

> *IF YOU WANT TO BE A LEADER, THE GOOD NEWS IS THAT YOU CAN DO IT. EVERYONE HAS THE POTENTIAL, BUT IT ISN'T ACCOMPLISHED OVERNIGHT. IT REQUIRES PERSEVERANCE.*
> *—JOHN C. MAXWELL*

What bolsters our perseverance? Faith! The Lord often allows us to experience more than we can handle on our own so that we will look to Him for help. He is *"the author and finisher of our faith"* (Hebrews 12:2 KJV). To us, it may feel like we are behind schedule, but as long as we continue to trust and follow Him, we will arrive at our destiny right on time.

God wants you to succeed!

Don't just move quickly past that statement. God *wants* you to succeed. You could even say that God has *created* you to succeed. And while there may be people all around you who either laugh or smugly nod their heads anytime you talk about your dream, remember to hang on to it. Declare to yourself over and over that our all-powerful, all-knowing, everywhere-at-once God wants you to succeed and will empower you to do so. The roundabout way is not a stop sign; it's a necessary part of the journey.

MARITAL AND FINANCIAL CHALLENGES

At Potential Church, the two challenges I most often counsel people on are marital and financial problems. When people are stuck there, they feel like they are in the weeds.

When you first get married, it's the two of you against the world. The hard times are behind you. You check off the boxes: Wedding...house...children—check, check, check! But it seems like many marriages get into trouble when the years pass by and stretch in front of you.

That lack of direction and attention can cause couples to get lost in the wilderness. They wonder if they weren't better off before. They doubt that they're on the right path and take a detour at Cheating Creek or Emotional Affair Alley, or abandon their partner at Lonesome Pass and put all of their energy into the kids.

But lonely marriages and difficult relationships don't happen overnight. They are the result of making multiple bad decisions over time. We forget that every decision we make takes us closer to our dreams or further away from them.

I smile to myself when I think of couples I know who "can't make it to church." They're too busy, they say. But when they have problems, boy, they have *got* to meet with me *that day!* They falsely believe that months or even years of bad decisions can be fixed in one counseling or prayer session. In reality, it is just the first of many steps. I have hope for every marriage, but it takes a troubled couple quite a while to get into the wilderness, and it's going take a while to get out. Couples get discouraged when I tell them that it's not about just one couple's weekend, a fancy dinner, or even spoken promises. It's about showing up, day after day, and repairing the damage that has been done.

GETTING BACK ON TRACK

You get back on the path of success the same way you get off it—*by making decisions.* But instead of doing what you want to do when you want to do it, you first ask a simple question: *What does my Creator want?* He is the one who set me free, He is the one I trust, and He is the only one who can safely get me to my destiny. His Word tells us:

> Trust in the LORD with all your heart, and lean not on your own understanding; in all your ways acknowledge Him, and He shall direct your paths. (Proverbs 3:5–6 NKJV)

Let's break this passage down. God lists three decisions that will get us back on track when we've allowed ourselves to get distracted while traveling the roundabout way.

TRUST IN THE LORD WITH ALL YOUR HEART

God's Word tells us what is true; therefore, we know what we should be trusting, what we should rely on. When we read the labels on food packaging, if we trust the company to be honest about its ingredients and the number of calories or carbohydrates, it can impact our decision to purchase or consume what's inside. When we trust the Lord with all our hearts, we lean upon His wisdom, found in His Word, to make decisions both big and small.

LEAN NOT ON YOUR OWN UNDERSTANDING

In 2007, when the first iPhones went on sale, I said they wouldn't last. "Blackberry owns the smartphone market," I confidently proclaimed. I was monumentally wrong, as was the wisdom I trusted to make that claim. I chose to miss out on experiencing what would become world-changing technology because I leaned upon my own flawed knowledge rather than trusting those who knew more than I did.

While it was disappointing to miss out on the first couple of years of iPhone hysteria, relying solely upon our own wisdom can get us into all kinds of trouble when making much more important decisions: Where should I work? Should I get married and have kids? Who should I marry?

How should I raise my kids? We all have opinions and gut reactions, but we should lean on the Scriptures and pray to God for guidance.

IN ALL YOUR WAYS ACKNOWLEDGE HIM

We often think only the *big* decisions matter. But the small steps we take every day will ultimately lead us back to the path when we have become distracted. As we acknowledge His wisdom for our lives, His authority over our lives, and His desire to see us succeed, we realize God's great love for us. It motivates us to trust, lean on, and acknowledge Him in all that we do.

"Good planning and hard work lead to prosperity, but hasty shortcuts lead to poverty" (Proverbs 21:5).

You should celebrate every small win—every day that you and your spouse stay together, every dollar saved, and every decision to deny your selfish cravings. There's a misunderstanding that finding yourself in the wilderness is only the result of bad decisions. And the roundabout way can be even more challenging than one major battle. But God is teaching you the same lesson He taught the Israelites. Faith that is built in the wilderness is stronger than the faith that is built in battle.

ROUNDABOUT SUCCESS STORIES

BREAKOUT HIT

In the early nineties, Robert Matthew Van Winkle—better known by his stage name, Vanilla Ice—was everywhere, appearing seemingly out of nowhere. His song "Ice Ice Baby" was the first hip hop single to top the Billboard charts. Actually, Ice's first love was motocross, but after breaking his ankle during a race, he worked on his breakdancing and rapping. Just two years after being discovered at a South Dallas nightclub, he released his first album. *To the Extreme* became the fastest selling hip hop album of all time, but Ice had to sign his life away to see it happen. The label pushed him to be more commercial, which led to a series of bad decisions. His movie, *Cool as Ice,* was a historic flop. It seems like as soon as he came on the scene, Vanilla Ice was gone.

Ice struggled in the following years. But over the next decade, out of the limelight—in the wilderness—he competed on a national level in jet skiing. He became passionate about real estate, got his contractor's license, and started flipping houses. His hit home renovation TV show, *The Vanilla Ice Project,* ran for ten years. He was Wellington, Florida's "Outstanding Citizen of the Year" in 2014. In 2020, his estimated net worth was $10 million.

ELEVEN HERBS AND SPICES

Harland Sanders, better known as Colonel Sanders, did not find success until he was sixty years old. As a young man, he practiced law—until a courtroom brawl with a client ended his career. He operated a steamboat ferry and sold life insurance and tires. It wasn't until he started serving meals to truck drivers in front of his Corbin, Kentucky, service station that he became well-known for his cooking. Once he could afford some pressure cookers, he perfected his quick frying "Kentucky Fried Chicken," coated in his secret recipe of eleven herbs and spices, and the rest is history. He sold the brand in 1964 for $2 million ($15 million in today's money) at the age of seventy-three.

TEN THOUSAND HOURS

Malcolm Gladwell is perhaps best known for the concept of the "10,000-Hour Rule." Gladwell is one of my favorite authors, and his best-selling third book, *Outliers: The Story of Success,* released in 2008, is an examination of the factors that contribute to high levels of success. In *Outliers,* Gladwell repeatedly cites the 10,000-Hour Rule, based on a study showing that the key to achieving world-class expertise in any skill is, to a large extent, a matter of practicing that skill for a total of 10,000 hours. As examples, Gladwell uses the Beatles, who performed live in Hamburg, Germany, more than 1,200 times before making it big, and Bill Gates, who spent 10,000 hours programming a computer he had access to starting in eighth grade. Gladwell also cites himself, noting it took him exactly ten years as a journalist to find success.

The secret to success, if there is one, is not genius, but perseverance. Sound familiar? On the road to success, there's really no way but the roundabout way.

> HARD WORK IS A PRISON SENTENCE ONLY IF IT
> DOES NOT HAVE MEANING. ONCE IT DOES,
> IT BECOMES THE KIND OF THING THAT
> MAKES YOU GRAB YOUR WIFE AROUND
> THE WAIST AND DANCE A JIG.
> —MALCOLM GLADWELL

The journey will take longer than you think, and it will feel even longer. You will feel lost at times. But trust that God is taking you on the right path. There's no going back. There's no quitting. If you trust God's plan for you and keep putting one foot in front of the other, you will reach your destiny.

WILDERNESS SURVIVAL GUIDE

Now that we see we're in the right place, let's look at some wayfinders that will keep us on the path so that we view preparing for our potential as progress.

REDEFINE PROGRESS

Since you now realize that success could take a while, let's create some small wins. Keep going! Some mile markers will allow you to see and feel real progress. Keep going!

When Steph and I loaded our three kids in the car in order to move to Florida in pursuit of our destiny, rather than progress, it felt a lot more like starting over. I had dreams of leading a young adult ministry at a large and influential church. True, Potential Church was large and influential, but I didn't start out leading a young adult ministry. As I've already confided, my first job was parking cars!

There is a three-letter word for what I was feeling: *ego*. In Arkansas, I owned a house; in Florida, I lived in a mobile home. In Arkansas, my wife was able to stay home with the kids, which was one of *her* dreams. But in Florida, she had to drop off our daughter at childcare and go back to work for us to just survive financially. In Arkansas, I was Pastor Troy, who had been a successful athlete and community leader. In Florida, people wondered, "Who is *he*?"

As I looked around at other pastors my age, it seemed they were raising more money and reaching more people. But as I look around twenty years later, it's easy to appreciate the journey that got me where I am today.

Where you are now doesn't determine where you will be tomorrow, nor does it have to. Your path is uniquely yours. Your potential is yours alone. Your measures of success should be uniquely yours as well. Whether it's another dollar saved, cupcake sold, or hour spent perfecting your jump shot, know that you are that much closer to your God-given goal.

STAY HUMBLE

You have a lot to learn! You will attain success, I promise you. But God's timing is the one to trust, not yours. *It's not just about getting there. It's about being prepared when you do get there.*

As I mentioned earlier, God doesn't want you to taste success then fail! Think about the professional athletes, entertainers, and CEOs whose hard work may have given them financial success but cost them their families. Maybe they accomplished their dream but lost their health. Success has a cost, and Scripture reminds us it is the wise person who counts it. Jesus warns:

But don't begin until you count the cost. For who would begin con-
struction of a building without first calculating the cost to see if there is
enough money to finish it?   (Luke 14:28)

When we are unprepared for all that success brings with it and begin
to believe our own press, that success could be our undoing.

Have you heard of ToyGaroo? I hadn't either. It was a toy subscrip-
tion service featured on *Shark Tank*, which raised $250,000 from investors
Mark Cuban and Kevin O'Leary. A "Netflix for toys" sounded like a great
idea,[5] and the investors were keen. But according to one of the founders,
Phil Smy, the company couldn't source the toys from manufacturers as
affordably as they had hoped. And not only that, they had promised "free
shipping," but because of the variety of toys, the shipping costs got out
of hand. With the spike in business caused by the TV show and public-
ity, coupled with the sourcing and shipping problems, the company went
under and filed for bankruptcy just a year after the episode aired. O'Leary
would later say that the company had a strong idea, but was "unable to
execute." They would have been better off growing slowly and organically,
working out the kinks over time.

Would you rather win the battle and lose the war—or the other way
around? God chose the latter for the Israelites. They were not ready for
the promised land. Success without first learning perseverance would have
been their undoing. By taking the long and roundabout way, they were able
to learn, experience small wins, and prepare for victory. They had to learn
it for themselves.

God did not leave the Israelites stranded in the wilderness. He guided
them with a pillar of cloud during the day and a pillar of fire at night. God
was going to show them where to go, but the problem, in their eyes, was
how long the journey was going to take. When it takes longer, costs more,
and is more difficult than we thought it would be, our attitude can get us
into trouble.

---

5. Phil Smy, "ToyGaroo: Burning $250K Building the Netflix for Toys," *Failory*, March 17,
2018, www.failory.com/interview/toygaroo.

While road rage isn't a new phenomenon, during the COVID-19 pandemic, it definitely spiked. We had two road rage incidents within five miles of my house. The anxiety of the pandemic was brought to the boiling point on the highway. What was supposed to be a trip to the mall ended up being extended to a prison sentence in one case and cut short in the other, as the driver lost his life.

> *THERE MAY BE PEOPLE THAT HAVE MORE TALENT THAN YOU, BUT THERE'S NO EXCUSE FOR ANYONE TO WORK HARDER THAN YOU DO.*
> *—DEREK JETER*

God doesn't intend to keep you in the wilderness! His timeline might not align with yours, but He will not forsake you or strand you there forever. Our confidence to arrive at our promised destiny is based upon the faithfulness of God to keep His promises, so remain positive, confident, and faith-filled.

TRUST IN THE LORD

Good pilots know that in bad weather, they can lose the horizon and think they are gaining altitude when they are really descending. Pilots who are unwilling to rely on their instrument flight rules can be surprised by the proximity of the ground when they clear the clouds; some have been known to fly their planes right into the ground.

However many pilots have had accidents over the years, that is just a fraction of the number of people who crash their businesses, ministries, and families into the ground. Rather than walking by faith, as we are encouraged to do in Scripture, they lead only from what they can see.

God's Word and the Holy Spirit will guide us around mountains and through turbulence if we will only trust Him.

Trust in the LORD and do good. Then you will live safely in the land and prosper. Take delight in the LORD, and he will give you your heart's desires. Commit everything you do to the LORD. Trust him, and he will help you. (Psalm 37:3–5)

LOST IN THE WILDERNESS

There are people who never leave the wilderness:

+ They live their whole lives stressed about money. They might even be wealthy by anyone's standards, but without trusting that the Lord will provide, comfort escapes them.

+ They turn back from their goal. How sad that the Israelites actually wondered *if they had been better off as slaves* rather than keeping their eyes on the road to the promised land!

+ They think there are shortcuts to success. They might fool others or even themselves for a time, but they never actually succeed.

You are not these people. God purifies what your heart desires as you travel on the roundabout way.

Pastor Rick Warren did not write *The Purpose Driven Life* until he was nearly fifty years old. The way he had lived his life up to that point had shown he could be trusted with success. *The Purpose Driven Life* sold millions of copies. Warren was able to leverage the influence and affluence that came as a result of such success into making a difference around the world while still enjoying his life. He got to a point where he now does what he calls "reverse tithing," giving away 90 percent of his income and living off 10 percent. He returned the twenty-five years of salary he had received before the book's success. I can't think of a better example of one's potential aligning with God's grace—that is, until I hear about yours!

The point to remember is that whatever success looks like, whether it is writing a book, starting a company, or beginning a family, you not only arrive in the promised land, but you enjoy life once you get there. It is the roundabout way that makes such a life possible!

QUESTIONS FOR REFLECTION

Can you think of a time when you felt like God was taking you the long way to success, but it actually turned out to be the right way?

Proverbs 3:5–6 (NKJV) says:

+ *"Trust in the LORD with all your heart."*
  Is there a decision you could look to God to help you with, whether through Scripture, your pastor, or attending church?

+ *"Lean not on your own understanding."*
  Write down some of your favorite inspirational scriptural passages or make a note of them on your phone.

+ *"In all your ways acknowledge Him."*
  What is one way that you could become more involved with your church, or passing on God's blessings to someone else?

Celebrate some small wins that you have had recently on the way to your vision. Then think of three next steps that you could take to reach it.

Think of someone you admire who took the roundabout way and experienced success late in life.

6

THE POWER OF RESISTANCE: UNEXPECTED OBSTACLES

When you believe you are on the right path, the roadblocks appear.

There's only one Michael Jordan. I have been a pastor for more than twenty years, but I have been a basketball player since I could toddle out to the court. Not a day goes by that I'm not in a pair of Air Jordans. They're my good-luck charms, so to speak.

In any kind of game, you *expect* opposition. It's not a game without it! You come to anticipate that you will be fouled, injured, delayed, or come up against a hot new player who will challenge your skills. In fact, that new player might even be on your team and angling for your position, so you'd better watch your back as well!

To be a successful basketball player, you practice your shot from every position on the court. You make sure you're in top physical condition because shortcuts won't cut it. You visualize yourself making a last-second shot or hitting a game-winning free throw. You listen to your coach and encourage your team—you might even put on your lucky Air Jordans! It is your preparation that prepares you for the obstacles that every athlete knows lie ahead.

IF YOU'RE TRYING TO ACHIEVE, THERE WILL BE ROADBLOCKS. I'VE HAD THEM; EVERYBODY HAS HAD THEM. BUT OBSTACLES DON'T HAVE TO STOP YOU. IF YOU RUN INTO A WALL, DON'T TURN AROUND AND GIVE UP. FIGURE OUT HOW TO CLIMB IT, GO THROUGH IT, OR WORK AROUND IT.
—MICHAEL JORDAN

Roadblocks are inherent to the game. In order to win, you must not only expect them but prepare for them. So I'm always a little surprised when people are stunned by roadblocks no matter what they are trying to achieve, whether in the game of leadership or life.

If you won't take it from me, take it from Michael Jordan: "There will be roadblocks....Don't turn around and give up." If someone else at work is up for that promotion, don't take your name out of the running. If someone knocks your business idea, keep going. If you get a bad grade, don't drop out of school. If you lack the resources to make your dream a reality, it's time to find a creative solution.

Many times when you are leading a team to make changes on the path to greatness, you will experience resistance or pushback, but keep moving forward. Once you have a God-given dream in athletics, in business, or in life, you have what it takes to win. The apostle Paul declared:

So let's not get tired of doing what is good. At just the right time we will
reap a harvest of blessing if we don't give up. (Galatians 6:9)

Now suit up and get out there!

2020 VISION: LIFE IS A JOURNEY

I have been on this journey at Potential Church for over twenty years—half as long as it took the Israelites to get the promised land. And I am coming to really and truly understand that halfway is not halfway there. The game could be lost at any point—down to the last second. But here's the good news: It could also be won!

In twenty-plus years at Potential Church, yes, I have come up against some roadblocks. Unexpected obstacles? Bless your heart! I have been fouled, injured, delayed, and challenged. But I have remained on the path, as hard as it is. I honestly believe that my years as a basketball player and coach were excellent preparation for the ups, downs, and pivots that are necessary to lead and minister to a congregation—or attain any goal imaginable. Kids, grab a ball and get dribbling!

But with over twenty years of preparation and experience under my belt, I never thought it was possible for me to be up against a challenge that could undo everything that God had used us to build.

ONTO THE COURT WALKED COVID-19

The pandemic changed the lives of every man, woman, and child in the world. It was a roadblock of biblical proportions for every goal, school, business, government—and church. It's not anything we did; we didn't cause it, and we could never have foreseen it. And as I write this, we are not through it. Perhaps you are still feeling the effects and sorrow generated by the COVID-19 crisis.

In those early months, my staff and I were in emergency mode, and the health, care, and feeding of our community were our highest priorities. At times, this seemed like more than we could handle. Everything else just stopped! Our Sunday services were cancelled at every campus; our school shut its doors. Any plans we had for 2020 were quickly shelved. The invisible enemy changed everything. Digital platforms, along with email and text, replaced Sunday services, school, small groups, lunches, and coffee huddles. I had to figure out how to lead, cast vision, and communicate hope through the lens of a camera. While all of this chaos was happening around me, I couldn't divorce myself from what was going on inside me.

And then in May 2020, George Floyd was killed, and decades of frustration, anger, and injustice boiled to the surface in cities and towns around the US. People were hurting, and the country was divided. We were in the middle of a pandemic, and if that were not enough, it was a presidential election year.

When you look at history, governments rise and fall, and powerful people come and go, but the church remains through chaos and pandemics, through persecution and corruption. So while there was no danger the church as a whole—the body of Christ—wouldn't survive 2020, there was the real possibility *our* church, Potential, wouldn't!

I can only imagine the immense responsibility Moses felt as he led millions of people through the wilderness to the promised land. Trying to determine the voice of wisdom was not an easy task. Moses sometimes listened to the wrong people and allowed fear to be the deciding factor, despite hearing from God. I didn't want to make the same mistake. Obstacles have a way of forcing us back to our foundational values and beliefs. We were determined to make decisions based on wisdom, not fear!

(By the way, there are three books in the Bible that are called its wisdom literature: Proverbs, Ecclesiastes, and Job. Respectively, these books teach us wisdom for successful living; the purpose and value of human life; and the problem of suffering and the doctrine of retribution.)

WE ARE ALL STARTING OVER

In time, as churches were allowed to reopen with socially distanced services, I gathered the staff of Potential Church and held the most important team meeting of my life. At this point on our journey, it didn't matter if I had been at Potential for two years, ten years, or twenty. The reality was, as a result of this crisis, *we were starting over.*

As with any unexpected roadblock or obstacle, however, we were faced with a choice. *Are we going to look at this as a setback—or as an opportunity? Are we going to quit or persevere? Are we going to focus on the problems or the solutions? Are we going to focus on the things we can control or the things we cannot control?*

I reminded my team that many of them had said in the past that they were sorry they'd never experienced being part of a launch. Well, now they were getting that opportunity!

As hard as I'd worked for twenty years—and many members of my team had been at Potential for almost as long—we had never seen so few people in our church. We were missing thousands of people. The size of the congregation had fallen to what it was twenty years before. We would be lying to ourselves if we thought they were all going to show up again someday. Because they were not. And as of this writing, they haven't all returned.

You may have been thinking the same thing about your business, your health club, or your wedding or birthday celebration. Sure, people were trickling in. But in all honesty, were we going to be able to see our journey through?

If you've never launched a church or started something from ground zero, you may not realize how much work and sacrifice it's going to take on your part. Getting a spacecraft off the launch pad takes a tremendous amount of energy, much more than is required to keep it in flight. The energy of a rocket is mainly expended when it's defeating earth's gravity. Similarly, the greatest amount of energy required to launch a plan comes at the beginning. It's called *productivity momentum.* Tasks become easier to do once you've started them—and that momentum will sustain you through this challenge and hopefully the next.

In life, in business, in ministry, and even in a family, you learn to live with imperfection and unpredictability. I never expect that my day won't include roadblocks. The only question is, what shape will they take? This is why the message of this chapter is so pertinent.

Whatever your vision for yourself was, on the path to your goal, you somehow neglected to prepare for roadblocks. Well, guess what? Here's your chance to start over!

JUST LIKE MOSES, FAIL OFTEN AND FAIL UP

Moses is often thought of as one of the most effective leaders who ever lived. Even people who don't necessarily believe in God think Moses was a great leader. But as we have learned, Moses made several very human mistakes—quite a few, actually. We are going to take a close look at five key ones so we'll be better prepared for the obstacles that are no doubt on the road ahead.

1. MOSES WAS IN A HURRY

When you get a nudge from God, there is a tendency to pursue your calling by getting ahead of Him. You're passionate, you're excited, and you're looking forward to reaching your potential.

Historians believe that Moses was being trained to become the next Pharaoh because the Egyptian ruler didn't have a son. As the adopted son of Pharaoh's daughter, Moses was in the royal family. As Stephen told the Jewish council, Moses *"was mighty in words and deeds"* (Acts 7:22 NKJV). Moses had probably led military campaigns. God had invested forty years in preparing him to be a leader—and ultimately to free His people.

And yet, as I mentioned in chapter 1, Moses killed an Egyptian and hid his body in the sand. God had raised up Moses to set His people free. But Moses was in a hurry.

A ruler has a right to rule. A judge has the right to punish you, but Moses had not earned these rights in the eyes of his fellow Hebrews. He was too hasty. Moses had his own ideas about the plan, but God's plan was different. So what did God do? God slowed him down. God took His time to prepare Moses—*forty more years!*

Remember that the next time you feel impatient—when the orders aren't rolling in, or you can't find a lease, or you're wait-listed at a school. *We are all on God's timing.* And believe me, in the end, that is the best time to be on.

I can't tell you the number of people I've known over the years who had a calling on their lives but got frustrated that the doors were not opening up quickly enough. They were in a hurry and made a bad decision. Had they been patient and waited just a few months, the opportunity that they were so passionate about would have made itself available. The door would have opened. However, the problem is that by the time the door did open, they were no longer there to walk through it. They had grown impatient.

When I was playing basketball in college, we had a talented point guard who had an athletic scholarship. He wasn't getting much playing time, so he became frustrated and complained about it. Eventually, he gave up his scholarship and quit the team. Just a few games after he turned in his jersey, our starting point guard was injured. If the other PG had still been there, he would have received more playing time than he knew what to do with. The door of opportunity opened, but he was no longer there. He was not the only one who missed out; the team also suffered because of his impatience.

MORAL: BE PATIENT

I can almost promise you that your vision will take much longer to accomplish than you believe it will. What is the key to a good shot in basketball? Be patient. Set it up. Look for the open player. It's good to be aggressive and be the one willing to take the winning shot, but take it too early, and you will miss the opportunity to win the game. Lack of patience cost Moses more than once. Life and leadership are all about timing.

EVERY STRIKE BRINGS ME CLOSER
TO THE NEXT HOME RUN.
—BABE RUTH

2. MOSES DRIFTED FROM HIS CALLING

In Hebrews 11:23, we learn, *"It was by faith that Moses' parents hid him for three months when he was born. They saw that God had given them an unusual child, and they were not afraid to disobey the king's command."* Moses's parents knew he had a calling.

But Moses grew impatient and messed things up for himself and those he was destined to lead one day. Moses needed time outside of the spotlight and away from the palace for God to prepare him for what lay ahead. He ended up in what must have felt like the middle of nowhere. He married, got a job as a shepherd, and made friends. His calling must have seemed like a long time ago in a place far away.

Rather than leverage his life as part of this preparation, he drifted from his calling. I can only imagine how long it had been since anyone had talked to him about his destiny or called him special as his mother did when he was just a child.

Then God shows up, in a burning bush of all things. (See Exodus 3:2.) This wasn't going to be as easy to ignore as the occasional news of what was happening to his people in Egypt. God reminds Moses He hasn't forgotten about the people of Israel or His intention for Moses to lead them to the land He had promised them.

And what was Moses's response to this incredible opportunity? *"Lord, please! Send anyone else"* (Exodus 4:13). Rather than seeing purpose behind everything he had been through, he in essence says, "Thanks, God, but no thanks!"

This is the same Moses who grew up in the palace of the most powerful leader in the world at the time. The same Moses who loudly spoke up for *his people* with both words and actions was now afraid to talk? Whether Moses was truly afraid or just using it as an excuse, we will never know. But what we *do* know is that God didn't accept his answer.

Moses's brother Aaron would speak to Pharaoh on Moses's behalf. But it didn't take Moses long to realize that while his brother may be a more effective speaker, when it came to leading the people, especially during challenging times, they wanted to hear directly from Moses.

In times of difficulty and challenge, like Moses, your team needs your resolve and confidence to lean on. If you and I aren't careful, we can give up on our destiny. We can give up on our dreams. We can start to believe that they're never actually going to happen. But if God's put it inside of our hearts and we're following Him, it's just on His timing.

Of course, it's always easier to *not be* who God created you to be, to get comfortable. Because who God created you to be is going to take effort and sacrifice. It's going to take work and struggle.

Even when playing my best, I would sometimes miss a shot. At times, I would be pulled out of the game and sit on the bench, wondering what I could have done differently. Most nights, the coach would once again look down the bench, walk over, grab me by the jersey, and say, "Get back in there!" And again, I would find myself wide open with the ball in my hands. If I hesitated, the defense would have time to respond. If I worried about missing the shot, more than likely, I would. But if I did what I practiced for hundreds of hours—rise into the air, body squared, eyes focused on the back of the rim, more times than not, *swish*, and I scored. My job was to put the ball in the basket, and in order to do that, I had to shoot!

MORAL: GET IN THE GAME!

There is very little pressure on the bench. No one is counting on you. The crowd isn't watching you. But you know the truth. It's time to get back in the game! You may not make every shot, but you will miss every shot you don't take.

> *SUCCESSFUL LEADERS SEE THE OPPORTUNITIES IN*
> *EVERY DIFFICULTY RATHER THAN THE DIFFICULTY*
> *IN EVERY OPPORTUNITY.*
> *—REED MARKHAM*

3. MOSES DIDN'T SET A GOOD EXAMPLE

Moses spent the first forty years of his life becoming who God created him to be. He was educated, and according to the ancient Jewish historian Flavius Josephus, he led the Egyptian army. He never forgot who God was, and he knew his calling in life. Then he got out on the backside of the desert, he married a Midianite, and he drifted from God.

I don't think any of us realize how easy it is to drift. But think about the impact of this drifting on the next generation. Moses, who was circumcised as a sign of God's covenant promise with the Israelites, had not even had his *son* circumcised! God confronted Moses and was about to kill him for this disrespect, when Moses's wife Zipporah stepped in. (See Exodus 4:24–26.) She was not even an Israelite and may not have wanted her son circumcised, but she realized its importance to God and took care of it. God relented, and so Moses lived.

When I became a father, I promised myself that I would never discipline my kids in anger. I wanted my discipline to always be for our children's future success, not my frustration. Learning to successfully lead ourselves is key to reaching our potential and a great example to set for our children.

But it was one of those nights. Steph and I had kept the kids up past their bedtime, so they were tired, as were we. On our way home, instead of a nice peaceful ride, the kids started to fight. "You touched me," one shouted. "No, I didn't!" another yelled. "Stop it!" "No, you stop it!" "You make me!" The noise coming from the back seat was stomping on my last nerve. Out of nowhere, I shouted at the top of my lungs:

"STOP IT AND BE QUIET!"

And quiet is all I could hear...for a moment. Then tears began to flow from all three children. Up until then, they had never heard me yell that loudly or with that much anger.

I had blown it. I had violated everything I had taught our children about anger, patience, and love. I had also broken the promise I made to myself to always discipline our children calmly and rationally. If you were to talk to Tyler, our oldest child, who is now twenty-nine, I'm sure he still remembers that night.

It's easy to become so focused on ourselves and what we have to do that we forget the importance of *being*. What we *do* may be forgotten by the next generation, but our attitude will be remembered.

You have to walk the walk. You have to set an example—for your kids, friends, coworkers, family, and teammates. If your goal is to be the first in your family to attend college, what happens if you give up? Your child learns to give up. After all, why should they work so hard to get good grades in order to go to college if you have not set the right example?

The apostle Paul says:

Throw yourself into your tasks so that everyone will see your progress. Keep a close watch on how you live and on your teaching. Stay true to what is right for the sake of your own salvation and the salvation of those who hear you. (1 Timothy 4:15–16)

MORAL: PRACTICE WHAT YOU PREACH

Leading by example may sound difficult, but it's actually one of the easiest ways to guide and motivate people. When we lead by example, our child, team, or staff has a clear picture of the path ahead and how to get there. They don't have to second-guess or suffer chaos, as Moses experienced when he neglected to circumcise his son. A leader who says one thing and does another is not a leader at all. A leader who practices what they preach will open doors for both themselves and their followers.

4. MOSES INVITED THE WRONG PEOPLE

The Bible says that when Moses and the Israelites left Egypt, they brought others on the journey to the promised land. Exodus 12:38 refers to them as *"a rabble of non-Israelites."* Egyptians and others went along, probably because the God of Israel had proven to be more powerful than the Egyptians' gods. These people were not committed to the vision, so it wasn't long before they began to complain—and those complaints were contagious:

> *Then the foreign rabble who were traveling with the Israelites began to crave the good things of Egypt. And the people of Israel also began to complain.* (Numbers 11:4)

When God calls you to do something great, you have to *surround yourself with greatness.* You might realize a week after hiring someone that they're untrustworthy or not a good fit, so you have to go through the whole process again. But you can't settle for people who aren't willing to make the sacrifice that will be necessary to accomplish the dream that is in your heart.

You have a responsibility to empower, teach, and equip your team to persevere through the journey. But if they're unwilling, don't bring them along, or you will regret it. When people aren't there for the vision, the promise, or the sacrifice, they become a problem. When Moses allowed some uncommitted folks to come along, important tasks were not completed, or they were done incorrectly. If you, as the leader, have to step in and make up the difference, that is not effective leadership. Are you motivated by the desire to see the task completed—or the fear of being found out that you made a bad decision in the first place? Either way, you will end up doing too much and be accused of trying to do everything yourself. Just like Moses.

In Exodus 18, we learn that Moses's father-in-law, Jethro, a wise man and a priest, hears of all that God has done for Moses, and he comes to visit him in the wilderness. Jethro sees that Moses is settling disputes among the people from morning until evening. Moses is doing everything!

> *"This is not good!" Moses' father-in-law exclaimed. "You're going to wear yourself out—and the people, too. This job is too heavy a burden for you to handle all by yourself."* (Exodus 18:17–18)

Moses needed to delegate—to teach, train, and trust in his people as well as pray for them. The key to success, whether in ministry, business, or family, is to raise people up. I hate to use this cliché, but *there's no "I" in team!* The people who succeed work their hardest to raise others up.

If you do it alone, you're going to burn out. Now you might say, "I don't have the personality for it. I'm not a people person. I'm not a good team player." I would say to you that there's not a successful leader, coach, CEO, pastor, or college dean out there who has not learned how to relate to and raise up his or her team.

There are as many personality types as there are successful leaders—quirky, brainy, outgoing, shy, conservative, risk-taking—but all of those leaders have placed an importance on bringing others along with them on the journey. If we want to have more students, clients, customers, or friends, then we have to grow as leaders.

I see leaders who are insecure, worried that their employees are probably going to do some aspect of their business better than they do, when they should be glad to have competent help.

It feels good to be needed and hear, "We couldn't do it without you! Thank goodness you were here!" However, leaders who are codependent are not doing themselves or their teams any favors. Ultimately, too much reliance on those being led leads to stagnation and a lack of productivity.

First Corinthians 9:27 says, "*I discipline my body like an athlete, training it to do what it should.*" The *body* often pushes against the very thing that will lead it to success because it doesn't feel good. We have to discipline our minds and recognize that raising up, empowering, and equipping other people will help both us and them reach our potential.

Moses took Jethro's advice. "*He chose capable men from all over Israel and appointed them as leaders over the people. He put them in charge of groups of one thousand, one hundred, fifty, and ten*" (Exodus 18:25). They settled most of the disputes among the people, bringing only the hardest cases to Moses to judge. In this way, Moses was not overwhelmed, and he brought up others with him. It was good for Moses, his leaders, and everyone else.

I'm not talking about raising people up to do what you don't want to do. I'm talking about raising people up so that you can be more successful at what God's called you to do, even if that means they get the reward or the pat on the back.

MANAGEMENT IS ABOUT ARRANGING AND TELLING. LEADERSHIP IS ABOUT NURTURING AND ENHANCING.
—TOM PETERS

MORAL: INVITE THE RIGHT PEOPLE

When Moses trained his ablest people to be leaders, then stepped back to let them lead, offering support when needed, both Moses and his people were empowered to move closer to the vision. As author Ken Blanchard warns in his book *Leadership and the One-Minute Manager*, we must be careful to choose the right people, not *seagull managers*—those who fly in, make a lot of noise, dump on everyone, and then fly out. Blanchard says, "The seagull style of management may be indicative of a manager who is untrained, inexperienced, or newly appointed."[6] As Moses discovered, inviting the wrong people along on the journey led to a bunch of squawking. Choosing leaders who emulated them would have made the journey even harder!

5. MOSES SECOND-GUESSED HIMSELF

In Numbers 13:2, the Lord tells Moses, "*Send out men to explore the land of Canaan, the land I am giving to the Israelites.*" When they return, these twelve explorers report, "*It is indeed a bountiful country—a land flowing with milk and honey*" (verse 27). But ten of them declare, "*But the people living there are powerful....We even saw giants*" (verse 28).

It is after this report that Moses loses confidence and starts to second-guess God's plan and promise. He totally ignores the words of Joshua and Caleb, who says, "*Let's go at once to take the land....We can certainly conquer it!*" (Numbers 13:30).

Moses did not relay God's wishes correctly because he himself second-guessed the plan. The spies' responsibility wasn't to determine *whether or not* they could go in; it was to determine *how* they were going to go in. And the spies said, "We can't do it!" Moses was leading by committee rather than leading with authority as a leader carrying the vision to reality.

There are always going to be people who tell you, "It can't be done" because discouragement and fear are among the enemy's most effective tools.

Hebrews 11:6 says, "*It is impossible to please God without faith.*" When a team is facing a great challenge, there will always be people who stand on

---

6. Ken Blanchard, *Leadership and the One Minute Manager* (New York: William Morrow & Co., 1985).

the sidelines, watching you do the work as they struggle with unbelief. But there will be the few, like Joshua and Caleb, who believe that the dream is possible—and they will be willing to work to make it a reality.

Moses had attempted to mix those committed to the vision with those just along for the ride. Without exception, the pessimists will pull down the optimists rather than vice versa.

In Gallup's 2017 study *State of the American Workplace,*[7] only 22 percent of employees strongly agreed that the leadership of their organization had a clear direction. I don't see that as a negative! It tells me there's tremendous room for growth, for leaders who can communicate a strong, clear vision to their team, ignoring the naysayers, doubters, and second-guessers. And there is no reason why one of those successful leaders can't be you!

IF YOU ACCEPT THE EXPECTATIONS OF OTHERS, ESPECIALLY NEGATIVE ONES, THEN YOU NEVER WILL CHANGE THE OUTCOME.
—*MICHAEL JORDAN*

MORAL: STICK TO GOD'S PLAN!

Have you noticed something about all of these obstacles that Moses faced? They were all *internal* obstacles! Moses's mistake, time and time again, was to waver from God's plan.

You will face difficulties on the road to your calling. They're part of the game. But they will only stop you when you put your human desires, needs, wants, or timing ahead of God's promise.

---

7. www.gallup.com/workplace/238085/state-american-workplace-report-2017.aspx.

Each of us has a destiny and a purpose. In challenging times, I often remind myself of God's promises in Scripture:

For I can do everything through Christ, who gives me strength.
(Philippians 4:13)

For we are God's masterpiece. He has created us anew in Christ Jesus, so we can do the good things he planned for us long ago.
(Ephesians 2:10)

Don't worry about anything; instead, pray about everything. Tell God what you need, and thank him for what he's done.   (Philippians 4:6)

Moses made mistakes. Michael Jordan made mistakes. And you and I do too. But don't give up. Accept these setbacks as chances to start over. Take a time out to rest, recover, and remember your purpose. Then get back in the game.

QUESTIONS FOR REFLECTION

The COVID-19 crisis required us all to start over in some way. How could you reframe as an opportunity some aspect of your life that changed as a result of the pandemic?

Think of a time when you acted hastily instead of methodically. What were the results?

Is there a situation in your life in which you've been stuck, and you know that now it's time to "get back in the game"?

It's important to bring the right people along on your journey. Have you ever let down your standards for your team or in a relationship? What did you learn?

7

THE POWER OF CONFIDENCE: DOUBT IS HUMAN, NOT DIVINE

Moses dealt with criticism and made some bad decisions.
Expect that you will as well.

Oh, the Israelites. They never failed…to fail! When they were slaves in Egypt, the Lord had told them that they were the children of God, and He would deliver them to the promised land. By bringing ten plagues on the Egyptians, He had forced Pharaoh to set them free. Led by Moses, they set out triumphantly on their way, protected by God with a pillar of cloud by day and a pillar of fire by night. The Israelites had no reason to doubt that they would arrive at the land of milk and honey.

But Exodus 14 explains that five days after leaving Egypt, the Israelites were camped in a valley. There were mountains on both sides with the Red Sea in front of them. The only way they could have left the valley was to go back the way they came—and from that direction, they saw Pharaoh thundering toward them, with his six hundred chariots and troops! Pharaoh had changed his mind about setting them free.

The Israelites were terrified!

GOD SETS AN AMBUSH

But this was an ambush that God set for Pharaoh. He knew that even though Pharaoh had let the Israelites go, he would have a change of heart. Pharaoh might believe that the ten plagues had been the limit of God's power. He would think that the Israelites were confused about the route and would be an easy target.

The Lord had spoken to Moses and laid out His entire plan in advance:

> *Order the Israelites to turn back and camp by Pi-hahiroth between Migdol and the sea. Camp there along the shore, across from Baal-zephon. Then Pharaoh will think, "The Israelites are confused. They are trapped in the wilderness!" And once again I will harden Pharaoh's heart, and he will chase after you. I have planned this in order to display my glory through Pharaoh and his whole army. After this the Egyptians will know that I am the LORD!* (Exodus 14:2–4)

God told the Israelites that He would save them while trapping Pharaoh. Though it might at times appear that they were in an unwinnable position, He would not desert them. In fact, He would prove His glory in such a final and certain way that the Egyptians would never threaten them again.

Even though the Lord had spelled out the plan for the Israelites, when they saw the Egyptian chariots' horses galloping toward them, they panicked.

> *They cried out to the LORD, and they said to Moses, "Why did you bring us out here to die in the wilderness? Weren't there enough graves for us in Egypt? What have you done to us? Why did you make us leave Egypt? Didn't we tell you this would happen while we were still in Egypt? We said, 'Leave us alone! Let us be slaves to the Egyptians. It's*

better to be a slave in Egypt than a corpse in the wilderness!'"
(Exodus 14:10–12)

They were only human. They were trapped, and their only means of escape was by sea. Their fear made sense. And indeed, when we find ourselves in a position that seems unwinnable, we should cry out to the Lord!

It's natural to doubt, even when we have faith. But did the Israelites, God's chosen people, really believe that God had brought them all the way out of Egypt to forsake them now? Their tone is galling. Their fear might be appropriate, but their mocking and their ingratitude were not. These were not words of faith or confidence in the Lord. Look at all of those questions they cried to the Lord. *Why? Why?*

When you are in a state of fear, remember the saying: *Never put a question mark where God has put a period.*

God told the Israelites exactly what He was going to do. There was no question. And yet, they questioned!

Have you reached a place in your journey to your vision where you feel backed into a corner, where the only way out seems like a dead end?

I hear fear in the bickering of married couples in crisis. I hear fear from the complaints of employees who are not climbing up the career ladder as quickly as they would like. I hear fear in the concerns of students halfway through college, worried about their student loans and not sure if they should continue. I hear fear in the cries of parents of children struggling with addiction.

On the face of it, it seems crazy that the Israelites would choose to return to slavery over continuing on what God had told them was the path to the promised land. But it's possible that, at this point in your journey, it doesn't sound crazy at all. Maybe you feel so stuck that you want to return to the life you knew, even if it was awful. At least you didn't have to make decisions, lead, or rally the troops!

FEAR SPREADS LIKE FIRE: LEADING BY EXAMPLE

FEAR IS THE PATH TO THE DARK SIDE.
FEAR LEADS TO ANGER. ANGER LEADS TO HATE.
HATE LEADS TO SUFFERING.
—*YODA*

I don't think it could have been said better than by everyone's favorite elder. In the *Star Wars* series—and I certainly hope you have seen these movies—Yoda was a legendary Jedi Master who was keenly attuned to the Force. This small, wide-eyed, wrinkled creature trained Jedi warriors, including Luke Skywalker, for more than eight hundred years, leading them to unlock the path to immortality. And he warned them, above all, not to be afraid.

You are the captain of this ship, my friend. You are driving the bus. You are leader of the pack, head honcho. You are never going to reach your goal without earning the faith of others. So once you sense doubt or fear in yourself, or especially in others, you must put a stop to it! You are going to have moments of fear, but to voice that fear and spread it among your followers is inexcusable.

During a challenging time in my own leadership, I called my friend Joel Osteen, and he reminded me to never let anyone see me sweat. It's okay to be afraid, but courage always moves forward.

The Israelites had been released from slavery in Egypt just five days before arriving at the Red Sea. They were not used to thinking for themselves. They probably thought that since they had been released from one master, they would just follow another, a better one—with none of the headaches. They could practically taste that milk and honey!

But for Moses to lead them like sheep to the promised land, not anticipating any roadblocks, doubts, commitment, or buy-in on their part? That was not going to work! They had to learn that their action and commitment were not only required but warranted. This was not just another god to blindly follow. This was the one and only God of all creation, and Moses was His emissary.

STICK TO THE PLAN: DON'T QUIT!

When you have played basketball for most of your life, the desire to dunk is only natural. In sixth grade, I sent away for a plan that was supposed to increase my vertical leap by twelve inches. I'm not sure the plan was capable of increasing hops, but there was a poem included in the materials that I have never forgotten:

Don't Quit

by Edgar A. Guest

When things go wrong as they sometimes will,

When the road you're trudging seems all uphill,

When the funds are low but the debts are high,

And you want to smile, but you have to sigh,

When care is pressing you down a bit,

Rest if you must, but don't you quit.

Life is strange with its twists and turns

As every one of us sometimes learns,

And many failures turn about

When we might have won had we stuck it out.

Don't give up though the pace seems slow—

You may succeed with another blow.

Success is failure turned inside out—

The silver tint of the clouds of doubt,

You can never tell how close you are,

It may be near when it seems so far;

So stick to the fight when you're hardest hit—

It's when things seem worst that you must not quit.[8]

Reading this poem, we can imagine the author standing next to some of the Israelites as the rumble of the Egyptian army's horses grows louder and louder with each passing moment. Turning to those around him, he reminds them:

So stick to the fight when you're hardest hit—

It's when things seem worst that you must not quit.

And if you listen closely, you too can hear those same words: You must not quit. Just like the Israelites, what you do next will have huge consequences for your future!

EVERY LITTLE THING GONNA BE ALL RIGHT

The Israelites were in a crisis situation. Yes, their options did not look good. But pay careful attention to what Moses told the Israelites to do in this moment, as it was one of his finest as a leader:

But Moses told the people, "Don't be afraid. Just stand still and watch the LORD rescue you today. The Egyptians you see today will never be seen again. The LORD himself will fight for you. Just stay calm."
(Exodus 14:13–14)

Moses summoned his courage to calm the people. It's very possible that he projected more certainty than he actually had! God had not told

8. "Success Is Failure Turned Inside Out," *Quote Investigator*, April 21, 2017, quoteinvestigator.com/2017/04/21/do-not-quit. Edgar A. Guest's original poem, entitled "Keep Going," was published in his *Just Folks* column in *The Indianapolis Star* on March 3, 1921. Some words have been changed over the years.

him *how* or *when* He would help. But in no uncertain terms, God had told Moses that He *would* keep them safe. So the Israelites' best option was to stand still and remain calm.

I bet you've found yourself here as well, proclaiming with absolute certainty to your children, staff members, friends, or family that, like the Bob Marley song, "Every little thing gonna be all right"[9]—when your fear or your doubt is raging inside you!

In his book *The Red Sea Rules*, author Robert J. Morgan writes, "God wants His children's emotions under control. That's hard for us. The very word *emotion* is the word *motion* with an *e* in front of it (for *erratic*, I suppose). Our feelings go up and down, sometimes with the velocity of a roller coaster....We have strong feelings, often driven by compelling circumstances. Yet all is worsened by giving our emotions free rein."[10]

Moses told the Israelites to *stop* and calm down. In doing so, they would prove their faith, and God would reveal His plan.

Why did God tell them to stand still? Because fear always makes us want to flee. The fight-or-flight response is a natural physiological reaction in humans and animals when they perceive a threat to their survival. The changes in the body—increased heart rate, blood rushing to the muscles, tunnel vision—are intended to give us increased strength and speed in anticipation of fighting or running.

When I wrote this book, COVID-19 put practically every leader in the world in fight-or-flight mode—from presidents and prime ministers to hospital executives, from school administrators to small business owners. The questions were endless: When do we end the lockdown? When can we reopen our business? How will we pay next month's rent? When will I go back to school? What will happen to us?

---

9. Bob Marley and the Wailers, "Three Little Birds," on *Exodus* (Island Records, 1977).
10. Robert J. Morgan, *The Red Sea Rules: 10 God-Given Strategies for Difficult Times* (Nashville, TN: Thomas Nelson, 2014).

When we're afraid, the natural reaction is, "I've got to get out of here!" But God told the Israelites, "Stand still. I have a plan." God was testing their faith.

Honestly, there was nowhere for the Israelites to run anyway. The Red Sea was in front of them, there were mountains on either side, and Pharaoh and his army were approaching from the direction they'd come from. There was no alternative but to stand still.

PUT OUT THE FLAMES: STOP, DROP, AND ROLL

After Moses stopped, as the Lord had commanded, he had a very human moment. He cried out to God—probably down on his knees, out of view of the people, quivering in fear. We don't know exactly what he did or said but we do know that God admonished him.

> *Then the* LORD *said to Moses, "Why are you crying out to me? Tell the people to get moving! Pick up your staff and raise your hand over the sea. Divide the water so the Israelites can walk through the middle of the sea on dry ground."* (Exodus 14:15–16)

It was time to *roll*.

Stop, drop, and roll is the phrase the nice firefighter who visited our grade-school classroom taught us to do if our clothing ever caught on fire. Rather than running around looking for water or help, the flames can be extinguished when you stop, drop to the ground, and then roll.

I find myself using a version of this three-part fire safety technique whenever I'm in deep trouble:

1. STOP MAKING EXCUSES

Are these legitimate fears, or is it just your *lizard brain* or the limbic system? That primitive part of your brain is responsible for fear, rage, hunger, and your sex drive. It's about all that a lizard has for brain function.

It just takes a moment for your lizard brain to give you a million reasons why you couldn't, wouldn't, or shouldn't do whatever you are perfectly capable of doing. Think of other times in your life where you missed an opportunity. Was it the right decision? Probably not. It was the emotional decision, and it felt right, even if it was wrong.

When it comes to our emotions, self-preservation isn't always the right decision. Author and screenwriter Steven Pressfield wrote for twenty-seven years before he got his first novel published, the bestseller *The Legend of Bagger Vance*. He has gone on to write nearly twenty more books and several screenplays. Pressfield calls our inner tendency toward self-sabotage, procrastination, fear, arrogance, or self-doubt our *resistance*. "You will NEVER, NEVER achieve your dreams until you learn to recognize, confront, and overcome that voice in your head that is your own Resistance," he says.[11]

Stop making excuses for wrong decisions and recognize the enemy's resistance. This will allow you to move forward despite your fear. By the way, this is called courage.

2. DROP AND ASK FOR GOD'S GUIDANCE

Drop to your knees and pray. Ask for God's guidance. Scripture tells us:

Tell God what you need, and thank him for all he has done. Then you will experience God's peace, which exceeds anything we can understand. His peace will guard your hearts and minds as you live in Christ Jesus. (Philippians 4:6–7)

God's guidance often comes through His words found in Scripture, but God also uses people and circumstances to give us direction. Ask for advice from a few trusted coworkers, friends, or mentors. Winston Churchill said, "When there is no enemy within, the enemies outside cannot hurt

---

11. stevenpressfield.com.

you." The still small voice of God's whisper is loud enough to give you the confidence to overcome your own *resistance* and change the world.

3. ROLL WITH IT!

Seth Godin, an entrepreneur and best-selling author of books like *The Dip*, *Purple Cow*, and *Tribes*, says one of his most important messages to startup businesses is, "Start shipping!" By that he means send the product or idea out into the world.[12] Take the next step. That design, product, artwork, or recipe is never going to be perfect. You might be criticized. You might make mistakes. In fact, it might get worse before it gets better. But you'll never know until you start shipping.

FOR EVERYTHING, THERE IS A SEASON...

Ecclesiastes 3:1 tells us, *"For everything there is a season, a time for every activity under heaven."* There is a time to reflect, a time to pray, and a time to act. The Lord opens the door to our potential. It waits on the other side, but we ourselves have to walk over the threshold.

James Levine, a professor of medicine at the Mayo Clinic, says, "Sitting is the new smoking." Sitting is bad for our health; it's motion that gives us energy, stamina, and confidence.

Sitting is bad for our mental health as well. Don't just sit there and fret about all of the things that scare you! *The secret to eliminating fear in your life is to move against it.* God says to Moses, *"Tell the people to get moving!"* (Exodus 14:15). Go for it. Step out and watch your fear vanish before your eyes. Faith is action.

I'm reminded of a story I heard from Chuck Colson, founder of Prison Fellowship, about a momentous day in the life of Larry Walters, a former truck driver who became a motivational speaker.

---

12. Seth Godin, "SHIPIT: A little pamphlet for people who can," seths.blog/2012/05/the-shipit-journal-now-in-free-pdf-format. Also see www.sethgodin.com.

One afternoon in July 1982, Walters tied forty-two helium-filled weather balloons to his lawn chair, thinking he would float fifteen or twenty feet off the ground and over his neighbor's yard. In case he went too high, he had a BB gun to shoot out a few balloons. Walters ended up sailing several thousand feet off the ground! He floated over Los Angeles International Airport, forcing air traffic controllers to reroute traffic. Eventually, Walters settled back down to the ground.

Later, he told reporters that he was scared during his flight, and he would not do it again. But why did he do it in the first place?

"A man can't just sit around," he said.

It's probably not a good idea to adopt Larry Walters' flying schematics, but how about his philosophy? You can't just sit there! Time to get moving!

A TOUGH ASSIGNMENT

In fourth grade, we had a substitute teacher for a week when Mrs. Johnson was at home with the flu. We had a cursive writing assignment for English, but since none of us liked writing in cursive and Mrs. Johnson wasn't there, the whole class wrote in print or block script.

Well, come Monday, Mrs. Johnson was back, and she wasn't happy. She yelled at us...at least it felt like that from my fourth-grade perspective. She told us that thanks to our unwillingness to follow directions, what should have been an easy A for everyone was going to be a B. But when I looked down at my paper, *I* had a C! So I went straight up to her desk and said quite sheepishly, "Mrs. Johnson, I didn't get a B; you gave me a C." Her reply was swift. "Well, you didn't even *print* well."

I'm telling you this story from more than forty years ago because my fear of writing has caused me to *stop* rather than *roll* when it comes to writing this book. Every time I would sit down to write, I would literally get sick to my stomach. For years, I allowed fear to keep me from acting on what I knew I was supposed to do. It was only when I stopped making excuses, dropped my fear, and went to God for direction and confidence that I began to hear for the first time what family and friends had said for years: "You can do this! You have a story to tell!" That motivated me to make a commitment and allowed me to fulfill it with the book that you now hold in your hands.

> *INACTION BREEDS DOUBT AND FEAR. ACTION BREEDS CONFIDENCE AND COURAGE. IF YOU WANT TO CONQUER FEAR, DO NOT SIT HOME AND THINK ABOUT IT. GO OUT AND GET BUSY.*
> *—DALE CARNEGIE*

THE TEST IS NOT OPTIONAL

God tested the Israelites in the way that He did—with chariots charging toward them and their only way out through the Red Sea—because tests of faith are not optional.

If you feel like you're in an impossible situation, you're probably right in the middle of the will of God. The challenges that you are going through are put there by God to prove His glory and test your faith in Him.

When my beloved Stephanie was pregnant with our first child, she was diagnosed with toxemia, a dangerous complication characterized by high blood pressure. She ended up in the hospital, and our son Tyler was born six weeks prematurely. There were times when I was afraid that I would lose them both. But God gave me the faith to continue to believe. God took care of Steph and blessed us with the birth of Tyler Holdyn Gramling. It was God's faithfulness during that time that has given me the faith to trust Him again and again even when things go crazy, like a worldwide pandemic.

Think about it. If you have no problems, then there's no need for faith in your life. If you have no problems, then you have no need for miracles. God told Moses and the Israelites exactly what He was doing, and yet they were fearful.

Your calling might be so clear to you. You've left the old life behind and are marching down the right path. You've taken some great people along with you. There still will be challenges and moments of doubt. It's human to be afraid and pause for a minute. But if you keep forging ahead and don't turn back, success awaits.

There will be many more tests on the path to our goals. God puts challenges in our way to prove His power. Sometimes they might seem like more than we can bear. But God does not put suffering into our life needlessly. Think of the greatest example in the Bible: the crucifixion of His own Son, Jesus Christ. Jesus was aware of His Father's plan for Him. In the Gospel of John, Jesus explains why He is willing to face death despite being fearful:

Now my soul is deeply troubled. Should I pray, "Father, save me from this hour"? But this is the very reason I came! Father, bring glory to your name. (John 12:27–28)

Jesus foresaw the agony that awaited Him. It was natural for Him to be afraid. But although He would be put in an impossible situation, He trusted that it was *the very reason* He had been put on this earth. He knew that His faith would bring glory to God, that His suffering would bring an eternity of glory.

While Jesus paid eternity's admission price—"*The wages of sin is death*" (Romans 6:23)—He asks us to trust Him and follow His example.

Anyone who wants to serve me must follow me, because my servants must be where I am. And the Father will honor anyone who serves me. (John 12:26)

Follow me. Serve me. These are *actions.* The Israelites thought God was going to do all of the work, but they were going to have to honor Him by believing in Him and that belief was going to demand action. Belief always does! Belief is different than hope. Hope can just wish for change. Belief is a verb that will always get us off the couch to act!

The Bible is full of examples of people just like you, facing the same kind of challenges. You can learn from their mistakes and be inspired by their successes. The God found in the pages of the Bible is the same God at work in your life today.

THE ONLY LIMIT TO OUR REALIZATION OF
TOMORROW WILL BE OUR DOUBTS OF TODAY.
—FRANKLIN D. ROOSEVELT

ONE SMALL STEP FOR MAN...

Let's return to those cornered Israelites in Exodus 14. They are hemmed in between two mountain ranges, with an army of Egyptians coming up behind them, ready to pounce, and the Red Sea stretched out in front of them. God has promised them that He will safely lead them out of this predicament. They're terrified, doubtful, even a little ungrateful! But Moses has gotten them to pause and gather themselves. And now just the smallest action on their part will save their lives.

God tells Moses, *"Lift up your rod, and stretch out your hand over the sea and divide it"* (Exodus 14:16 NKJV). These were simple instructions connected to a mighty miracle. In the same way, the greatest miracles often happen with simple actions on our part.

And the LORD opened up a path through the water with a strong east wind. The wind blew all that night, turning the seabed into dry land. So the people of Israel walked through the middle of the sea on dry ground, with walls of water on each side!　(Exodus 14:21–22)

Moses's rod or staff did not part the sea; it connected him with God's saving miracle.

Do you see how just the smallest action toward your goal, toward staying on the path, will connect you with God's grace?

We all know how this story ends: the Egyptians chase the Israelites onto the path between the parted sea waters, but God throws Pharaoh's army into confusion to delay them. After the Israelites are all safely on the other shore, at sunrise, God tells Moses to raise his rod again. This time, the waters rush back and drown the Egyptians. Not one of them is spared.

...ONE GIANT LEAP FOR MANKIND

I just love the story of the parting of the Red Sea. It illustrates so clearly, like your grandma told you, "The Lord works in mysterious ways." He protects us, and He empowers us.

Here's something to think about: In this story, the Lord is not only showing us the path to the promised land, He is actively clearing it of enemies as well. God sets up an ambush for the Egyptians and erects a pillar of cloud that shrouds them in darkness. Then *"just before dawn the LORD looked down on the Egyptian army from the pillar of fire and cloud, and he threw their forces into total confusion"* (Exodus 14:24). This gives the Israelites more time to cross the parted waters.

If you are a child of God, He is always working to keep you safe. You might not always see it or sense it, but it is happening.

Sometimes we are so concerned with our own vision that we don't even notice how the struggles of two weeks ago seem like ancient history. This is one of the reasons I journal—so I won't forget just how often God has parted the Red Seas in my life.

God could have easily performed these works—confused the Egyptians, parted the waters, and closed them back up again—without help. Moses did not have to lift his staff for the Israelites to be safe. But by commanding Moses to do that and have the people march across the Red Sea, God was revealing to them their faith in His power to provide. They would need both His power and their faith in Him where they were going. Scripture says God's power can move mountains even if our faith is as tiny as a mustard seed. (See Matthew 17:20.)

In other words, God led you into this tough spot, and He will lead you out. But you will have to do the walking.

GOD HELPS US IN SMALL WAYS TOO

Miracles like the parting of the Red Sea do not happen as often as we would like in life. However, God also helps us in quite ordinary ways.

Don't expect your competitor's restaurant to be struck by a lightning bolt, your tuition money to fall from the sky, or Mr. Right to knock on your door. God will challenge you. But He will protect, guide, and provide for you. Start paying attention to the little wins. Just keep putting one foot in front of the other, and you will be amazed at how far you end up going.

How sweet the song of deliverance that Moses and the Israelites sang once they were safely across the Red Sea:

I will sing to the LORD, for he has triumphed gloriously; he has hurled both horse and rider into the sea. The LORD is my strength and my song; he has given me victory. This is my God, and I will praise Him—my father's God, and I will exalt him! (Exodus 15:1–2)

Deliverance came to the Israelites, and it awaits you as well. But you must confront, sit with, and then push through those very human emotions of doubt and fear. In times of crisis, you must act. *Step* toward your potential, *sing* His praises, and *exalt* in Him. God will give you strength!

QUESTIONS FOR REFLECTION

Have you reached a place in your journey to realize your vision where you feel backed into a corner? How will you move forward from there?

Don't Quit is a poem that has inspired me since I was a child. Is there an inspirational poem that you identify with? Make a point of keeping it close to you.

I keep a journal so I won't forget just how often God has parted the Red Seas in my life. Try keeping a journal for a month to see if you notice patterns and recognize God's gifts.

STEP THREE:
COMMUNITY

8

THE POWER OF CONNECTIONS: HELP FROM SURPRISING SOURCES

Moses often received support from unexpected people.
Pay attention, and the same will propel you toward your destiny.

Do you ever find that some ideas are so basic, it's difficult to define them? You just know it when you see it.

That could be said of *common sense*. *Merriam-Webster's Dictionary* defines it as "sound and prudent judgment based on a simple perception of the situation or facts."

Notice it says a *simple* perception. You don't have to go to Harvard, or be a doctor, an engineer, a grown-up, or even a pastor to recognize common sense in a person.

The Golden Rule is common sense. "Do unto others as you would have them do unto you" seems self-explanatory.

COMMON SENSE IS NOT SO COMMON.
—VOLTAIRE

Problems arise when we forget to use our common sense or give in to our fears. A common sense perspective requires getting outside of our insecurities and our doubts and trying to *understand each other* when we disagree. But in this day and age, are we really trying? It's so much easier to stay in our comfort zone and surround ourselves with people who agree with us and don't challenge us.

You are trying to lead. You are trying to treat others as you would like to be treated, give your customers the service you yourself would enjoy, and honor your spouse as you would like to be honored.

But that means communicating, understanding, anticipating—in other words, a lot of hard work. And really *listening*, not just to your friends and family but also to those who might not agree with you, who might even compete with you. Perhaps this is why common sense seems to be in such short supply today. Often, inaction comes down to fear and complacency.

One of the lessons of leadership is that you can't do it on your own; you must raise people up with you. And if you can manage to overcome your fear, your ego, and your insecurities and really listen to those around you, common sense will make itself available to you.

FINDING LESSONS IN OBSTACLES

Scripture has so many valuable lessons that apply to our lives today. But if you want to succeed in life, there's no better person to study than our old friend Moses on his journey to the promised land. God has created you with a destiny, a dream, a purpose. Moses's story is filled with insight on how to stay on the path, but it also contains examples of how you can drift from it. We have already covered many of them, but there's still much left for us to learn from him.

On the journey to the promised land, there is adversity. There are enemies. There are crises. But there are lessons in those obstacles. Instead of keeping you from your destiny, they can actually propel you toward it. These experiences are intended to help, not hurt you. God was guiding Moses, and He is guiding you too. But you have to pay attention. Otherwise, you will misread propellants for obstacles and run from what you should be embracing.

We are used to looking for guidance from the usual sources, such as a boss, a parent, a teacher, or a friend. But in this chapter, we will seek help from advisors that we normally wouldn't expect. If we use common sense, we would consult a wide range of sources to make better decisions. But as we have established, common sense is in rare supply today!

FOUR SURPRISING C'S OF SUCCESS

Therefore, if you can humble yourself to keep your ear to the ground, what you will hear might surprise you. Here are four surprising sources where Moses found guidance that are normally overlooked.

1. COMMON COMPANIONS

Throughout Moses's life, he received help over and over from people who were ignored or discounted in society. And first among these were *women*. At the time of Moses, women were considered to be less intelligent, inferior, and even the *property* of men. In reality, they often proved themselves to be the ones with more wisdom and courage than the men around them!

Moses, one of the Bible's greatest leaders, would have died or been killed several times over if it were not for women. We have already discussed how Moses's wife, Zipporah, saved him from God's wrath, but in fact, women had been protecting Moses from the moment he was born. Pharaoh had ordered the midwives in Egypt to kill all newborn Hebrew boys, but Shiphrah and Puah disobeyed the edict, honoring God's wishes by letting Moses live. Obedience to God often demands courage.

Moses's mother, Jochebed, knew there was something special about her son, so she hid him at home for three months. When it was no longer safe to do so, she placed him in a little ark among the reeds along the bank of the Nile River. She trusted him to God's care, a courageous act.

Moses's older sister, Miriam, then follows her baby brother along the riverbank to make sure he is safe. Although she is merely a slave, when Miriam sees that Pharaoh's daughter is going to find Moses and rescue him, she bravely runs up and asks, *"Should I go and find one of the Hebrew women to nurse the baby for you?"* (Exodus 2:7). Thus she manages to have Moses nursed by his own mother! Pharaoh's daughter goes on to persuade her family to protect and adopt Moses—no small feat. The Egyptian royal family accepts this Hebrew child, and he receives a prince's training and education, which serves him well when he eventually unseats Pharaoh himself.

Remember all of these lessons the next time you second-guess a *woman's intuition*! God wants us to listen to those whom society considers to be *inferior* or *invisible*.

You can also get covert advice from *your employees*. When was the last time you checked in with your employees at every level? Walked their walk?

The Emmy Award-winning show *Undercover Boss*[13] secretly put top executives of major companies to work alongside their lowest level staffers. The heads of companies like 7-Eleven, White Castle, and Waste Management toiled away in convenience stores, commercial kitchens, landfills, warehouses, and other venues. In most cases, they learned how backbreaking or difficult the work was. Some of these executives were even fired by on-site managers! In every case, these leaders walked away with knowledge, insight, and humility, having learned more about how to make their company succeed. "Management by walking around," as many have called it.

Even the person in your high school yearbook who was termed the *least likely to succeed* could have insights for you.

---

13. *Undercover Boss*. Created by Stephen Lambert. CBS, February 7, 2010–April 8, 2022.

I was often overlooked when I played basketball competitively. Although I was considered tall in high school, being a six-foot-four white guy is not exactly a good bet for professional basketball. I looked up the statistics. In the National Basketball Association, 70.4 percent of the players for the 2022-2023 season were African-American. In National Collegiate Athletic Association Division I men's basketball, 52.8 percent of the players were African-American.[14] And six-foot-seven is the average height to earn a college hoops scholarship!

It was really easy for coaches and players to discount my ability to make a difference. I was passed up by a lot of teams. But despite the odds, I did have some success. In 1988, I was Honorable Mention All-American. Though many college scouts may have doubted my skills, I did my best to exceed their expectations, and I was successful as a player and a teammate. The college coach who risked a full scholarship on me was rewarded, and I helped lead our team to a conference championship. I was also offered a contract to play in Europe.

Very few leaders, if any, would think that those who saved Moses had the power or possibility of saving *their* lives. How do you put this lesson into action? Who are the overlooked people in your life? Is it the client who makes small purchases but buys often? One of your students? A coworker? Your spouse? The person who cleans your office? Don't walk past those who are bypassed by most people, and you will gain insight and wisdom.

Who are those folks in your sphere of influence? Remember Moses before you ignore your employee's idea, or fail to take an email from your staff seriously, or ignore your child at the dinner table. It's common sense… that is often the sense that makes a difference.

2. COMPETITION

One of my favorite books by one of my favorite authors is *Team of Rivals: The Political Genius of Abraham Lincoln* by the historian Doris

---

14. *The 2023 Racial and Gender Report Card: National Basketball Association* and *The 2021 Racial and Gender Report Card: College Sport*, the Institute for Diversity and Ethics in Sport, www.tidesport.org.

Kearns Goodwin. It's about one of our country's most respected leaders, Abraham Lincoln. This book carries a wealth of leadership lessons, but one of the most unexpected is that Lincoln staffed his presidential cabinet with not just like-minded politicians and friends but his rivals.

In 1860, the prairie lawyer and former one-term congressman stunned the country by surpassing three prominent politicians—former New York Governor William H. Seward, Ohio Governor Salmon P. Chase, and Missouri lawyer Edward Bates—to win the Republican nomination for president. Then, after being elected, Lincoln did something even *more* surprising. He appointed Seward as secretary of state, Chase as secretary of the treasury, and Bates as attorney general. The president won over these former enemies with political genius, emotional intelligence, and self-confidence. They became his supporters and friends and helped him steer the country through its darkest days.

In explaining his decision, Lincoln said:

We need the strongest men of the party in the Cabinet. We needed to hold our own people together. I had looked the party over and concluded that these were the very strongest men. Then I had no right to deprive the country of their services.

The Bible says we should love our enemies. (See Matthew 5:44.) Moses's enemy was Pharaoh, who wanted to kill him. In the long run, however, Pharaoh's own daughter was responsible for her father's defeat. She saved Moses, who was used by God to ultimately set the people of Israel free and destroy the army of Egypt.

But *love your enemy* doesn't mean *lose your mind*. Moses's mother didn't put her baby in the river and just walk away. She sent her daughter to follow the basket to make sure that Moses was okay. I'm sure she even knew what time Pharaoh's daughter typically came to the river to bathe. We still need to be careful about how we progress, like Moses's sister Miriam was.

Abraham Lincoln did not surrender power to his rivals. Instead, he appreciated and absorbed their wisdom. He took the long view and kept the country's greater good in mind. He didn't surrender his common sense; he leveraged it for his success as well as our country's.

THE IMPORTANCE OF A NARRATIVE

Competition drives us. It's human to be concerned about the competition, but it's foolish to be paralyzed by it. If we pay attention, it can teach us huge lessons. In ministry, we are in competition for people's time, energy, passion, and resources. Every organization is asking us to get involved and help. Every business that produces a product or service wants our money. One of the things I've learned from our *competition* is the importance of a narrative.

Just check out any of the high-end fashion lines like Louis Vuitton, Gucci, and Chanel. They will assure you that you're not just purchasing a leather handbag, but an item that has a history and has been handcrafted by artisans for quality and sustainability. By purchasing one, you become part of the story. It's just a handbag at the end of the day, but the narrative makes it feel like so much more.

The church, on the other hand, has a legacy that goes back thousands of years. People have given their lives so others could be part of its mission. The church introduced public education and built the first hospitals; our *product*, the gospel, has the power to transform lives.

I've learned from my competition that people are looking for a story that matters, and they want to be a part of it. We've always had the story, but our competition reminds us that we need to tell it!

It's not about recycling your competition's success; it's about learning from them. It's easy to point out their mistakes, but what are they doing that's succeeding? What does your competition have to teach you? If you can leap over your fear and insecurity and have a little humility, your competition can teach you quite a bit! It's common sense.

3. CRITICS

You have probably learned by now that achieving your potential takes both a willing heart and a thick skin. Criticism is a constant on the road to success in business and in life. Often it is given with good intentions; sometimes it is not! But if you can learn to discern between constructive feedback and sour grapes, you might actually learn to appreciate your critics' lessons.

Sometimes you should be just as suspicious of praise as you are of complaints. As Norman Vincent Peale said, "The trouble with most of us is that we'd rather be ruined by praise than saved by criticism." Is that true in your life?

Criticism creates tension inside of us. It challenges us to question or investigate. Was it a good decision? Were our motives pure? Did we act arrogantly? The tension of criticism is uncomfortable, so if we are not careful and intentional, we will shut it down. I'm not saying we need to spend hours evaluating every critical comment on social media, but we need to be willing to be comfortably uncomfortable. To reach our potential in what we are pursuing is to invite the tension that comes from criticism.

THE DREAD OF CRITICISM IS THE DEATH OF GENIUS.
—WILLIAM GILMORE SIMMS

MORE ON THE GIFT OF SELF-AWARENESS

There were many times when the Israelites criticized Moses on the road to the promised land. In fact, it was criticism that had sent him on his journey to Midian as a young man. As discussed earlier, after Moses killed the Egyptian and hid his body in the sand, a fellow Hebrew called him out on it the next day. Moses was terrified; he thought he might be killed by Pharaoh for what was ultimately a sin and a crime.

But if we think about it, the man who questioned Moses's actions saved his life. In a way, he helped Moses become self-aware. Self-awareness is one of the most important gifts that God can give us in all of our relationships. Moses didn't respond, "Well, hey, he was beating that guy up," or, "I'm just trying to help you out." No. Moses understood that his actions had been hasty and shortsighted. He had gotten ahead of God, and he was in big trouble—life or death trouble!

Business guru Tom Peters often says, "Fail forward." We will all make mistakes on the road to our potential. Oftentimes, others will point these mistakes out to us. When we think no one's looking, someone is.

As we discussed in chapter two, it's important to decide who to listen to when determining right from wrong. It's common sense. Our critics can be a surprising help to us because they may have information we lack, but not everyone's opinion is valid. We can discover which people we should listen to through discernment.

Moses was criticized regularly and often by the Israelites. They questioned everything, including the route, the food, the weather, and his leadership. At times, this criticism drove him to seek God for answers and support, which led to positive outcomes. But there were also times when rather than deal with the tension that criticism brings, resulting in growth, Moses responded in frustration and failed to follow God's instructions. The cost was always high:

> *There was no water for the people to drink at that place, so they rebelled against Moses and Aaron. The people blamed Moses and said, "If only we had died in the LORD's presence with our brothers! Why have you brought the congregation of the LORD's people into this wilderness to die, along with all our livestock? Why did you make us leave Egypt and bring us here to this terrible place? This land has no grain, no figs, no grapes, no pomegranates, and no water to drink!" Moses and Aaron turned away from the people and went to the entrance of the Tabernacle, where they fell face down on the ground. Then the glorious presence of the LORD appeared to them, and the LORD said to Moses, "You and Aaron must take the staff and assemble the entire community. As the people watch, speak to the rock over there, and it will pour*

out its water. You will provide enough water from the rock to satisfy the whole community and their livestock." So Moses did as he was told. He took the staff from the place where it was kept before the LORD. *Then he and Aaron summoned the people to come and gather at the rock. "Listen, you rebels!" he shouted. "Must we bring you water from this rock?"* **Then Moses raised his hand and struck the rock twice with the staff,** *and water gushed out. So the entire community and their livestock drank their fill.* (Numbers 20:2–11)

The people were able to drink water that day, but because Moses allowed their criticism to frustrate him to the point of *hitting* the rock instead of *speaking* to it, God did not let him enter the promised land. (See verse 12.) Let that be a lesson on your journey!

Criticism can be used to help us become more self-aware in the areas we need to grow or mature in. But if not handled correctly, it can cost us our future. Like Moses, many a leader has foregone their potential over a few moments of frustration.

4. CRISIS

As Winston Churchill was working to configure the United Nations after World War II, he famously said, "Never let a good crisis go to waste." I thought about this quote many times during the COVID pandemic. When faced with adversity, people often want to just escape it, or numb themselves to it and pretend it's not happening. They binge-watch a show on Netflix and chill out with a bowl of ice cream or popcorn.

But crises reveal your preparation. Boxing legend Joe Frazier once said, "Champions aren't made in the ring, they are merely recognized there." At Potential Church, the COVID crisis revealed how prepared we were as a church. It tested our social media communication, community outreach, and leadership flexibility. But it also prepared us for an uncertain future and strengthened us for the next crisis that comes our way.

Our very human tendency in a crisis is to get into fight-or-flight mode—and flight sure sounds good! But when faced with COVID, I dared to ask myself, "What do I know about a crisis?" I thought, "I'm going to get to discover who I am. I'm going to get to discover how I deal with anxiety. Do I have faith? Do I have conflict? I'm going to get to understand if I've prepared over the last few years."

I often think of James 1:2–4 (NIV):

Consider it pure joy, my brothers and sisters, whenever you face trials of many kinds, because you know that the testing of your faith produces perseverance. Let perseverance finish its work so that you may be mature and complete, not lacking anything.

Trials lead to perseverance. In the midst of a crisis, you may find yourself thinking, "This is not fair. Where is God? Why is this happening to me?" But what we discover in the story of Moses is that these tests propelled him to where God was taking him.

God has not changed—He is *"the same yesterday, today, and forever"* (Hebrews 13:8; see also Malachi 3:6). He works in our lives in the same way He did for Moses. So when crises come, if we stop and think it through, we'll actually be surprised by the benefit that they can play in our lives.

LIFE IS A LABORATORY FOR ASKING WHY

Not all of us grow up in a house with positive role models. In fact, sadly, many of us experience challenge, failure, and stress. It's perfectly natural to wonder whether you're going to be able to overcome those obstacles in order to succeed.

Take marriage, for example. I was born when my mom was young, and my dad was in the military. When I was about twenty-five, my parents separated. While they both sacrificed for me and my two brothers, they struggled to get along. Like too many families, there was a lot of frustration, anger, crying, and even yelling at times. Were the *fun* times we had as a family worth all of the painful times? Were my fiancée, Steph, and I destined to go down the same road? Would our relationship look the same?

Some people never marry because their parents didn't stay together. All they saw and experienced was hurt and pain.

It's natural to doubt whether you're going to be able to succeed when you look around and see failure. You get a new job, and you think you're going to struggle because your parents were never able to get very far in life or their careers.

I am here to tell you that you can succeed even if those around you have not. Are your experiences going to impact you? Of course. But you are going to have to overcome your fear in order to reach your potential. Remember that this is the uncontainable power of God within you. He's placed this dream, this vision, inside you and wants you to achieve it.

There are things we can learn from our experiences that we often try to forget. When I reflect on the relationship my mom and dad had and the pain and hurt our whole family experienced, I ask a deeper question than whether all marriages are destined to end eventually. I ask why. Why did my mom and dad struggle so much? If you were to ask anyone about either of them, you would get glowing reviews. My dad worked long hours to provide for our family. He taught me to have a strong work ethic and never give up. My mom sacrificed in every way for me and my brothers. She took me to church from the time I was in her womb and talked to me about dating and its effect on one's future.

Why did these two people who impacted my life in such a positive way struggle in their relationships with each other? The answer to that question has helped my marriage to Stephanie become the most fulfilling relationship in my life.

You may be experiencing a challenging environment. You may assume that if others have struggled or even failed while going through the same thing, you will too. But instead, why not think of it as an opportunity, a laboratory in which you get to ask the question, "Why?" Using the scientific method of observation, discover what tools will help you reach your potential.

It's easy to think that your challenges are so great, there's no way in the world for you to be able to succeed and go to law school, start a business, have a successful ministry, build a strong marriage, or raise competent children.

But every proficient person you know came from a messed-up family—because no family is perfect. And it's important to work through that to create something better. If you don't, the cycle will continue. Those who did not reach their potential will be the very ones who are making decisions for you, and it will mess you up.

Sir Isaac Newton's third law of motion states that for every action, there is an equal and opposite reaction. I'm a pastor, not a physicist, but I do observe this phenomenon in the world of emotions. As awful as your role models may have been, you can be equally that amazing. The only way you will fail in life is to give up on the dream that God has put in your heart.

James 1 instructs us to persevere. What leads to success? Perseverance. Don't grow weary in doing things well because in due season, you'll reap a bountiful harvest—if you don't give up. (See Galatians 6:9.)

Every good marriage occurs when the couple does not give up. Every great parent didn't give up. Every amazing business founder didn't give up. Every growing church didn't give up. The circumstances had no bearing on it; you can find successful people in authoritarian countries as well as ones in which people are free and thriving. Maybe one is more challenging than the other, but the outcome depends upon how true we are to the promise that God has given us to keep.

FIND CONFIDENCE IN EVERY CHALLENGE

Look around. Put your ear to the ground. Ask for help and not just from the normal sources—it is all around you! It's common sense.

God gave you the gifts, the talents, and the desires to realize your dream. You think He's going to keep you from it? I hate to tell you, but the very things you fear are the very things that will help you take that next step.

You probably don't think of common people, competitors, critics, and crises when you are looking to find help, or as steps on the road to success. But that is the miracle of God's promise. In every challenge, there is confidence. Don't let it go to waste.

QUESTIONS FOR REFLECTION

The Golden Rule, "Do unto others as you would have them do unto you," seems like common sense, but sometimes, you have to remind yourself. When has it proved useful in your life?

When have you received advice or been inspired by the example of someone who is normally overlooked?

What is something you have learned or could learn from your competition?

Critics challenge us to question or investigate. When was a criticism you received a constructive one?

What have you learned from experiencing a crisis in your life?

9

THE POWER OF STRUGGLE: THE BATTLES CONTINUE

Just because you have had a breakthrough doesn't mean there aren't more struggles—but they will only strengthen you.

When all the people had crossed the Jordan, the LORD said to Joshua, "Now choose twelve men, one from each tribe. Tell them, 'Take twelve stones from the very place where the priests are standing in the middle of the Jordan. Carry them out and pile them up at the place where you will camp tonight.'" So Joshua called together the twelve men he had chosen—one from each of the tribes of Israel. He told them, "Go into the middle of the Jordan, in front of the Ark of the LORD your God. Each of you must pick up one stone and carry it out on your shoulder— twelve stones in all, one for each of the twelve tribes of Israel. We will use these stones to build a memorial. In the future your children will ask you, 'What do these stones mean?' Then you can tell them, 'They remind us that the Jordan River stopped flowing when the Ark of the LORD's Covenant went across.' These stones will stand as a memorial

among the people of Israel forever." So the men did as Joshua had com-
manded them. They took twelve stones from the middle of the Jordan
River, one for each tribe, just as the LORD had told Joshua. They car-
ried them to the place where they camped for the night and constructed
the memorial there....The armed warriors...led the Israelites across
the Jordan.... These armed men—about 40,000 strong—were ready
for battle, and the LORD was with them as they crossed over to the
plains of Jericho. That day the LORD made Joshua a great leader in the
eyes of all the Israelites, and for the rest of his life they revered him as
much as they had revered Moses. (Joshua 4:1–14)

WHAT KIND OF A PARTY IS THIS?

Let's review what just happened in this passage from Joshua 4. When
the Israelites crossed the Jordan River after forty years in the desert and
finally reached the promised land—when they essentially achieved their
ultimate goal—what happened next? Did God rejoice? Was there a grand
celebration? Was there high-fiving? Were there bubbling fountains of milk
and honey?

Not exactly!

Through Joshua, God commanded His chosen people to:

+ Pick up twelve stones to represent each of the twelve tribes of
  Israel.

+ Pile them into a memorial for future generations.

+ Pitch camp.

+ Prepare for battle!

Not only that, but you'll also notice something else: Moses is no longer
with them. He has died before even reaching the promised land! His
assistant, Joshua—who is not a young man either, being somewhere in his
seventies—is charged with leading the Israelites across the Jordan River.
Despite being the Lord's servant for forty years and delivering His people

out of slavery to the Egyptians, Moses will not enjoy the success of having reached the promised land. Instead, he dies within view of his goal.

You call this a victory lap?

But in fact, the Israelites' experience of what one would term *success* might be much closer to your experience after reaching your goal than having a celebration, eating cake, and feeling pleased with yourself. You're in college now? Great! You've beaten your sales goals? Fantastic! You got that promotion? Congrats!

And then you realize: Now you have to *go* to college. Reach *higher* sales goals. Actually *lead* this team at work. Now the real work begins.

I recognize this feeling, as I have it every Sunday afternoon, if I'm lucky. After a week spent writing and then delivering a sermon I'm happy with, ministering to the congregation, and encouraging the ministry teams without incident, I'm ready to celebrate! Have some ribs, play with my grandchildren, watch some sports.

And then I remember: There's another Sunday coming down the pike! I've got to do what I just did all over again! And it often feels like I'm starting from scratch, which means I'd better get back to my desk sooner rather than later.

Moses was our flawed but dutiful leader on the path to success. We have learned from both his strengths and his frailties. But now we will learn from his successor, Joshua, about the right and wrong things to do in order to step into our success.

Success itself can be very hard to handle. When you are in pursuit of your goal, you have your team and a shared purpose. It gets you out of bed in the morning and fuels your dinner-table conversations. But when you enter into the land that was promised, what happens next?

God's instructions to Joshua are not busy work or artificial hurdles. He is fortifying His chosen people with some tools to handle what happens when, at long last, they cross the river into their promised land.

WHEN SUCCESS IS SQUARE ONE

Success can be its own challenge; it takes the same commitment but different, elevated skills. Now is not the time to take your eyes off the prize. From God's instructions to Joshua and the Israelites, we learn four important lessons about how to move on after success.

1. STAY HUMBLE

After each and every Israelite has crossed into the promised land, God directs the leaders of the twelve tribes to go back to the middle of the Jordan River, collect a stone, and pile them up so they will *"stand as a memorial among the people of Israel forever"* (Joshua 4:7).

I appreciate that God's first instruction after success is to take some time to appreciate, metaphorically and tangibly, the weight of what has happened. These memorial stones will remind their children and their children's children that they are living in the promised land because of the efforts of their forebears.

> *THOSE WHO CANNOT REMEMBER THE PAST*
> *ARE CONDEMNED TO REPEAT IT.*
> *—GEORGE SANTAYANA*

Have you heard the expression, "Some people are born on third base and go through life thinking they hit a triple?" Right off the bat—no pun intended!—God is reminding His chosen people that their success was borne on the shoulders of others, and their success will serve as a memorial to future generations. That future success is the result of faith that doesn't surrender to fear, even to giants.

TEAMWORK MAKES THE CAR GO ROUND

Some say great wisdom only comes with age, but I disagree. In fact, I had one of my greatest epiphanies when I was just nine years old. I could barely cross the street by myself, but I had a mental breakthrough that caused me to see the world through a completely different lens. And it came from a very unlikely source: NASCAR.

When I was growing up, my hometown in Arkansas was crazy for NASCAR. My neighbors were fanatics for the drivers. They could tell their favorite car out of the dozens that flew around the track each weekend, watching on the small, square television sets that flickered in living rooms up and down my block. I was never really into the sport as much as the kids at school. When the topic of the latest NASCAR race came up with my friends, I'd always want to bring up my favorite part of the race, which they found a little unusual. It wasn't who won or who wrecked—it was the pit stops. I was fascinated when a car darted into a pit stop to have the tires changed and gas tank filled. I remember staring open-mouthed at the screen as the five-person pit crew jumped over the wall and serviced the car in such a timely and efficient manner. It was the epitome of teamwork.

That realization started me on a way of thinking that changed my life. The driver's main job is to drive fast and turn left. He has to keep the car on the road as other drivers attempt to pass and avoid accidents at all costs. When it's time to service the car, the driver signals his crew chief and steers into the pit. A pit crew may include up to twenty people with different tasks, utilizing different skills. Someone changes the front tires, while another changes the back tires. Still others jack up the car, add fuel, carry the tires, wash the windshield, and more. They all have the same goal: getting their car across the finish line first.

My mom used to say that TV would ruin my brain, but as I watched a pit crew one day, I was struck by the fact that while the driver may get the glory after the win, it was the team that made it happen. I think of that pit crew often.

When accolades come your way, it's important to remember that your success is not only shared but depends on your crew. You may not always remember the name of the person who changed the tires, but without them, you are not going to get very far. I've experienced the power of team on the basketball court and in the church. There is nothing more humbling or fulfilling than pursuing a dream so big that it's impossible to accomplish on your own.

FAILURE IS NOT SO MUCH A PHYSICAL STATE AS A STATE OF MIND; SUCCESS IS FALLING DOWN—AND GETTING UP ONE MORE TIME—WITHOUT END.
—JIM COLLINS

HOW THE MIGHTY FALL

After studying how great companies were made, resulting in bestsellers like *Good to Great* and *Built to Last*, in 2009, best-selling author, speaker, and consultant Jim Collins and his research team put their energies into determining why successful companies fail for his book *How the Mighty Fall: And Why Some Companies Never Give In*. They identified five stages of decline of successful companies.[15] See if any of these sound familiar:

1. Hubris born of success (arrogance, entitlement)

2. Undisciplined pursuit of more (overreaching, obsessed with growth)

3. Denial of risk and peril (blaming, refusal to face facts)

4. Grasping for salvation (panic, desperation, silver bullets, star CEO recruits)

---

15. Jim Collins, "Five Stages of Decline," www.jimcollins.com/concepts/five-stages-of-decline.html.

5. Capitulation to irrelevance or death (leaders abandon all hope of building a great future or sell out)

Though Collins identifies five stages of decline, it all comes down to that first word: *hubris. Merriam-Webster's Dictionary* defines it as "exaggerated pride or self-confidence." When we're feeling cocky and take our eyes off the ball, things start to slip. As Proverbs 16:18 warns, *"Pride goes before destruction, and haughtiness before a fall."*

One day while I was having lunch with William Vanderbloemen, founder and CEO of the Christian executive search firm Vanderbloemen, he shared that his company had noticed in their research that a church often plateaued when their senior leadership reached the average age of forty-five. Whether you're a church leader or a business leader, I can't help but wonder if Jim Collins's research reveals some of the reasons why. If you plant a church in your twenties and that church is still around in your forties, you have beaten the odds, overcome numerous challenges, and experienced what most would consider to be success. Yet there is no doubt that the very things you have worked your whole life for—stability, community, impact, and legacy—can lead you down the path Collins describes.

Look at King David, a man Scripture calls a man after God's own heart. (See 1 Samuel 13:14). In his success, David forgets this—and essentially forgets why he is king. The Bible says:

In the spring of the year, when kings normally go out to war, David sent Joab and the Israelite army to fight the Ammonites. (2 Samuel 11:1)

David didn't go to war; he stayed at the palace to chill and do the 1000 BC equivalent of bingeing on Netflix. He did discover a beautiful woman to spend his time with; problem was, she was married. In fact, Bathsheba just happened to be married to one of the men King David had sent to war.

When Bathsheba got pregnant with David's child, everything began to fall apart. His arrogant attempt at a coverup led to embarrassment, murder, and the eventual death of the baby. While we may not often think of humility as a key to success, as Jim Collins discovered and King David experienced, pride and arrogance are sure to lead to downfall and failure!

2. SET BIGGER GOALS

SUCCESS SEEMS TO BE CONNECTED WITH ACTION. SUCCESSFUL MEN KEEP MOVING. THEY MAKE MISTAKES, BUT THEY DON'T QUIT.
—CONRAD HILTON

Are you feeling a nagging loss of purpose after reaching your goal? Finishing your home renovation, completing the marathon, signing the contract, winning the championship? Well, you are not alone. After the Israelites create this twelve-stone memorial, they are instructed to pitch camp. There's no castle waiting on this side of paradise, no garden of Eden, and no honey milkshakes. It's a night like any other: pull out your tents, start a fire, pitch camp, and rest for the night. More battles await tomorrow.

Besides NASCAR, another thought I had when I was nine while watching TV was wondering if I could play in the NBA. I was a basketball player and dreamed of reaching the highest levels of the sport from the time I could walk. My dream seemed unlikely, but not entirely impossible.

You already know the answer. Still, I remain fascinated by professional basketball players and other professional athletes to this day. And not only what happens to them at the highest levels of sports, but what happens to them afterward. Every minute of these athletes' lives has been mapped out—every workout, meal, and moment of activity or rest. These elite competitors function as part of a team, with a small army of coaches, chefs, agents, and others also working toward an elusive championship. So what happens after they get atop that podium, feel the weight of that trophy, and ride in their hometown parade, dabbing their tears on their jersey...and their career ends? What's next?

TREAD WATER OR KEEP SWIMMING?

Well, often not a lot. Many of these go-getters find that their "get up and go has got up and went." Olympic athletes, even those who win the coveted gold medals, find themselves confronted with unfamiliar and often terrifying thoughts of the future after spending years training in their sport. Many former Olympians struggle with depression, obesity, and addiction, not to mention financial problems and a general lack of direction.

It's such an issue that the US Olympic Training Center in Colorado Springs has a program in place that helps athletes translate the goal setting and planning that brought them to this extraordinary level of their sport into developing themselves outside of it.

Michael Phelps, possibly the greatest swimmer who has ever lived, participated in his first Olympics at just fifteen years old in 2000 and retired after his fifth Games, the Rio Olympics in 2016, having won his twenty-eighth and final medal. He is the most successful and decorated Olympian of all time.

But out of the water, Phelps faced grave personal struggles. A photo of him smoking marijuana went viral, and he was arrested twice for driving under the influence. At one point, Phelps has said, he did not even want to live.

How did he pull himself back from this dark place? By setting some new goals.

Not only did Phelps return to swimming and compete in two more Olympic Games after a brief retirement in 2012, he had successes in other fields. He founded the Michael Phelps Foundation, devoted to growing the sport of swimming and promoting healthier lifestyles. In 2020, he co-produced and narrated a documentary for HBO called *The Weight of Gold*, which explored the struggles of Olympians during and after their competitive careers. Today, Phelps is sober, married, a father of three, and devoted to promoting physical and mental health. He has redefined success for himself.

What will be your next goal? Will it be more of the same, setting new benchmarks, or be a different goal entirely? One could say that Michael Phelps pursued all three: more medals, beating his own records, and trying to spread a positive message through both nonprofit work and film production.

What have you not had time for as you started your business? What book should you write? What new idea should you pursue? Could your business have a global impact, or should you diversify into other areas? What could you do to fuel your next success?

3. WORK HARDER

PEOPLE WHO SUCCEED HAVE MOMENTUM.
THE MORE THEY SUCCEED, THE MORE
THEY WANT TO SUCCEED,
AND THE MORE THEY FIND A WAY TO SUCCEED.
—TONY ROBBINS

When comedian Jay Leno got the coveted job of hosting NBC's *Tonight Show* in 1992, he deposited his (huge) paychecks right in the bank. For decades, he continued to live off his income from doing comedy gigs on the side and never looked at how much he was saving. "You know, when you start making money, you get lazy. I wanted to make sure I always had that hunger, so I never looked," he told CNBC's show *Make It*.[16] After twenty-two years as *Tonight Show* host, he accumulated "a nice little nest egg," he adds. Leno

---

16. Kathleen Elkins, "How Jay Leno went from earning minimum wage at McDonald's to making millions hosting 'The Tonight Show,'" June 15, 2018, CNBC *Make It*, www.cnbc.com/2018/06/15/jay-leno-went-from-mcdonalds-to-making-millions-at-the-tonight-show.html.

still does stand-up comedy, explaining, "If you do something and it works, then keep doing it."

Church pastors are part of people's lives at every stage. Over and over again, I have watched people retire or slow down...only to give up. It's incredible to me the number of people who work their whole lives in order to have enough money to retire. They often lose a sense of purpose and their health after only a few years of retirement.

A study of Shell Oil employees found that those who retired at age fifty-five and lived to be sixty-five had a 37 percent higher risk of dying than those who retired at sixty-five.[17]

I've got news for you. If Jay Leno, at age seventy-four, is still working nights, I don't care what level of success you have attained, you still have opportunities to achieve more!

NEW GOALS, NEW PLAYBOOK

You have a commitment to yourself, your team, the people who helped you reach whatever level of success you have, and those you are inspiring by your example. People are paying attention. The stakes are raised. Your level of performance needs to rise to meet them.

God attempted to teach this to the Israelites with His next instructions to Joshua. After they build the memorial and pitch camp, God has the Israelites craft flint knives and circumcise all of the sons of Israel who had been born in the wilderness—none of whom had been circumcised over the past forty years.

After telling Joshua and the Israelites to prepare for battle, why would God slow them down now to circumcise all of the menfolk, which would incapacitate their army for many days? It didn't seem to make sense!

God is taking this moment when He has performed miracles to capitalize on their faith and renew His people's faith and obedience to Him. The people

17. Shan P Tsai et al., "Age at retirement and long term survival of an industrial population: prospective cohort study," *British Medical Journal*, October 29, 2005, www.ncbi.nlm.nih.gov/pmc/articles/PMC1273451.

who died in the wilderness were not the same body of people who were entering the promised land. These people were free of the slavery mentality of those who fled Egypt. They are not the slaves of the past but God's people.

It would not be a lack of armies or armor that hobbled the Israelites' future success, but a lack of commitment to the Lord and to their goals.

It's time to take a breath, reflect on your life, and remember that God has been with you up to this point and will not leave you now or ever. If you are truly going to discover and live a life of purpose, it begins with Him. Not just an acknowledgment and a head nod or eye wink, but a commitment.

Every commitment you make begins with a surrender, a willingness to give up a certain set of ideas and fully pursue your purpose. It means surrendering the pursuit of self to commit to something much greater. And your purpose, like mine, is found in a person: Jesus Christ. There are many pursuits in life you can commit to, but I have discovered for myself and seen in the lives of thousands of others that there is only one worthy goal for us: the pursuit of and commitment to Jesus Christ. You might be surprised at the number of people who have discovered their potential after surrendering their lives to Christ.

4. EXPECT THE HATERS

CRITICISM IS PROOF THAT YOU'RE ON THE RIGHT TRACK. I KNEW EARLY THAT THE MORE COMPETITORS BADMOUTHED ME, THE MORE SUCCESSFUL I WAS BECOMING.
—BARBARA CORCORAN

I love this 2019 tweet from Barbara Corcoran.[18] She's one of my favorite judges on the ABC TV show *Shark Tank*. I love her frank talk and her

---

18. twitter.com/barbaracorcoran/status/1212176908336664577.

brutal honesty, but I also love the story of her rise to the top of the business world. Corcoran always seems polished and confident, but she comes from humble beginnings. She grew up dirt poor and aimless, received all Ds in high school, and went through twenty jobs by age twenty-three. A boyfriend loaned her $1,000 so they could start a real estate company, but they split seven years later when he married their assistant. Still, over the next two decades, Corcoran persevered and built a real estate empire. In 2001, she sold the Corcoran Group for $66 million. She went on to join the *Shark Tank* panel in 2008 and published the bestseller *Shark Tales: How I Turned $1,000 into a Billion Dollar Business* in 2011.

Today, Corcoran is worth $100 million and married with two children. She fully believes her difficult childhood made her who she is today and continues to fuel her drive. She was the second oldest of ten kids. Her dad often drank too much, couldn't keep a steady job, and treated her mom disrespectfully. Corcoran vowed that no one would ever talk down to her that way.

Corcoran might not allow people to talk down to her, but that doesn't mean she isn't the target of criticism nearly every day. Though she has everything she ever wanted and more, she still struggles with the constant shots in the media about her TV advice, the way she ran her business, and her appearance. It still hurts, but it only adds to her drive.

Jealousy. Criticism. Office politics. Competitors. Gossip. In Paul's letter to the Ephesians, he notes, "*We are not fighting against flesh-and-blood enemies, but against evil rulers and authorities of the unseen world, against mighty powers in this dark world, and against evil spirits in the heavenly places*" (Ephesians 6:12).

When you reach a certain level of success, you know that more is possible. Therefore the battle is not against physical barriers but spiritual ones.

DEALING WITH CRITICS

If Barbara Corcoran is bothered by her critics, chances are you will be too. If jealousy or office politics are getting you down, take a deep breath and try these techniques:

- *Don't take it personally.* Criticism often says more about the critic than the person who is subjected to it. It might take everything you have, but try kindness, especially to yourself. As I mentioned earlier, you have to predetermine who you will listen to and who you will not. While it is important to be kind to everyone, it's impossible to take everyone's criticism or advice at the same level.

- *Don't apologize.* Being the boss means making tough decisions. Sadly, it's usually the end of being *one of the guys.* You can explain your actions, but you don't have to feel bad about them.

- *Confront the whispers.* Be direct and open; your actions will set a good example. Listen and try to understand.

After the Israelites crossed the Jordan River, Scripture says, "*The Lord made Joshua a great leader in the eyes of all the Israelites, and for the rest of his life they revered him as much as they had revered Moses*" (Joshua 4:14).

Joshua demanded much from God's people and for that, they *revered* him. Leadership means making hard choices, thinking bigger and smarter, and keeping your head amid both praise and criticism. The trust of your people is the ultimate reward!

QUESTIONS FOR REFLECTION

When have you thought you had reached the *promised land,* only to find out your work had just begun?

Think of people in your family, in your business, or in your life who have helped you succeed. How can you honor their place in your life?

Setting bigger goals can mean more of the same or a different objective. What is the next benchmark in your life?

How can you align God's Word with your purpose just a little more closely?

10

THE POWER OF LEGACY: TRUE SUCCESS IS A SUCCESSOR

Potential doesn't end with you.
Help others rise up and reach their potential as well.

Go for it!

I worked for my dad during the summers when I was a teenager. My official title was *gofer*—the assistant, not the animal. I was the one who would "go for" whatever my dad needed—a hammer, a wrench, a cup of coffee, whatever.

My dad was a master electrician, but also did plumbing, heating, and air conditioning. In other words, he did a little bit of everything. And in the midst of getting the *stuff* that was necessary for him to complete a job, I learned what to do with that stuff, such as how to install a toilet, wire a light switch, and run ductwork. It wasn't until I got married and moved several thousand miles away after college that I realized just how many skills had been passed down to me. Steph and I didn't have the money to pay someone to fix the toilet or install a ceiling fan. I *had* to do it, and here's the thing: *I could!*

Good leadership isn't what happens when you're around; it's what happens when you're *not there*. Good leaders pass down skills to their followers, just like my dad did for me.

Take the example of Moses and Joshua. Joshua started as a gofer, just like I did. But Moses chose Joshua for a reason. And on the journey to the promised land, Moses taught Joshua the skills he needed to become an effective leader. Why did Moses choose Joshua? And how did he train him? Let's take a look.

YOUR TIME IS FLEETING

You might be thinking, "I've just read this whole book on discovering, sharing, striving for, and achieving my potential, and now you want me to hand over the reins to someone else?!"

Well, maybe not today, maybe not tomorrow…maybe not for years. But I want you to understand that there will come a day when the enduring family, organization, or business you have created will need a new leader. You will have to turn it over to your successor. I believe that one of the reasons God did not have Moses lead the Israelites into the promised land is to emphasize the point that leadership is temporary.

Leadership is temporary. Let's think about that concept for a minute.

In Deuteronomy 31:2–3, before the Israelites crossed the Jordan River, Moses told them:

> I am now 120 years old, and I am no longer able to lead you. The LORD has told me, "You will not cross the Jordan River." But the LORD your God himself will cross over ahead of you. He will destroy the nations living there, and you will take possession of their land. Joshua will lead you across the river, just as the LORD promised.

Note that though he was a hundred and twenty years old. Moses was not ceding his position because he was old or weak. He still climbed to the top of Mount Nebo after this speech! But Moses was the only leader God's people had known. God did not want His people to put undue faith in Moses. He wanted them to understand that whoever led them, He would be right beside them, and everything would unfold according to His plan.

Often, we wait until it is too late to empower our people. It's pretty routine to see a business take a hit once the founder leaves, or for our kids to struggle a little once they're out on their own. And training a successor is hard work! We might have a few false starts. Not everyone we raise up is going to be our successors; people move to other places and other jobs. We might get frustrated, hurt, or disappointed. We might just think, "Forget it! I'll just go back to doing everything myself!"

But God living in your heart gives you the courage to take on a risk to provide for the next generation, to think beyond yourself. You have to be intentional, and it has nothing to do with whether you're a great leader or not.

Scripture says there was no leader like Moses. (See Deuteronomy 34:10.) And yet Moses began to look for successors very early on. He relied on Aaron, on Hur, on Jethro, and others, but Joshua was the one who ended up leading the Israelites into the promised land. Moses first chose Joshua to lead their men to fight the army of Amalek. (See Exodus 17:9.) He brought *his assistant* Joshua to climb up the mountain to receive the Ten Commandments, and Joshua witnessed Moses's anger when he smashed the two tablets after seeing the people worshipping the golden calf. (See Exodus 24:13, 32:17–19, respectively.) Joshua was also present at the Tent of Meeting in which God spoke to Moses face to face. (See Exodus 33:11.)

Through all of these important milestones in the history and journey of God's people, Joshua is present, witnessing and learning. He has been empowered by God and by Moses to succeed him as a leader.

Is this something that you, as a leader, can humble yourself to do for the betterment of your family, your organization, your business? Succession isn't something that you start to think about as you age. Families, organizations, and businesses will only live beyond you if from the day your child is born, you get a promotion, or you open the company doors, you intentionally and humbly pour into and raise up the next generation.

IN SICKNESS AND IN HEALTH

Just as I put the finishing touches on this book, I was forced to reflect on this lesson in a very real way—from a hospital bed. Only a few weeks before this writing, I struggled for air and recorded short videos on my iPhone for Steph, my three children, and the members of Potential Church, in case I did not survive. In spring 2021, just as life was getting back to *normal* after a year and a half in COVID-related lockdown, we were preparing for a big homecoming Mother's Day weekend at Potential. Vaccines were readily available, and we were going to schedule our appointments. Finally, more families would be able to return to the church and worship together!

And then I got COVID. I was sicker than I have ever been in my life. I couldn't breathe or walk when I was admitted to the hospital. For the first three days, I had four doctors visiting me twice a day, with varying degrees of bad news. Double pneumonia was just the start of it.

As I lay alone, unable to see my family, only hospital staff clad in personal protective equipment, I reflected on the last time I had received bad news from doctors. That was 2006, when I was only thirty-nine years old. Back then, I was short of breath, and when I exercised every morning, I would feel an ache in the side of my neck. I didn't get much sympathy from the other pastors or even Steph. After all, I was too young to have any serious issues. But a few months later, after an angiogram, even the cardiologist was surprised to find some blockage. He said it was possible that my heart would "just explode." Three stents and a few weeks later, I was back on my feet.

In 2021, lying in my hospital bed, I reflected on one major difference between this health crisis and the last one. Back then, I was ashamed to admit that I was terrified of dying. My children were young, Steph and I were happy, and Potential Church was growing. I was worried that everything would fall apart without me...and I was afraid of the act of dying. This was not good! To fear death discredited everything I had taught my whole life. One of my favorite scriptural passages comes from Paul's first letter to the church at Corinth:

> *"O death, where is your victory? O death, where is your sting?"... But thank God! He gives us victory over sin and death through our Lord Jesus Christ.* (1 Corinthians 15:55, 57)

One of the greatest benefits of the good news is that we can face death without fear! With COVID, I went from being well to being unable to breathe so quickly that I really had no idea whether I would live. But I was at peace with death. Why?

I thought of Craig Groeschel's brilliant book *Chazown: Discover and Pursue God's Purpose for Your Life*. In chapter one, entitled "Your Final Chapter," he writes:[19]

Most people take a long time to die.

(This is no way to start a book, you say.)

But think about it. There are those few who go suddenly....But for you, chances are that at the end of your life, you will die in bed. Waiting.

And while you wait, you will very likely have days, weeks, even years to think, to look back on your life.

Groeschel's book inspired me to live each day making decisions that would give me peace at that very moment, lying in bed, at risk of dying. Moses's example had informed me as well.

19. Craig Groeschel, *Chazown: Discover and Pursue God's Purpose for Your Life* (Colorado Springs, CO: Multnomah, 2017).

I took stock of my life.

I didn't want Steph to be lonely, or my kids to lose their dad, but we had built a foundation within our family that would outlast me. The kids would support their mother. I felt a peace about the strength of our family, of the example we had set in the past, and the hard work that we had done.

I felt confident in my team at Potential Church, especially after enduring the peaks and valleys of COVID over a year and a half. We had put systems in place. My family and assistant pastors understood the message. I had raised up people around me who could continue Potential's mission.

I was concerned that my death would cause the congregation to turn their backs on God. Why would He take their pastor? But just like Moses had been empowering and engaging Joshua for forty years, I had brought people up by giving them opportunities and responsibilities that mattered and enabled them to succeed.

As I recorded all of these messages on my iPhone from my hospital bed, I was blessedly at peace. As awful as it was, one of the lessons of COVID was that it allowed us as individuals to realize that many of us are scared to death of *death*. It was beside us, next door to us, and affecting our families, our friends, our coworkers, and our acquaintances.

Of course I didn't want to die! I still had work to do. I thought of the structures I wanted to create in all the areas of my life, of the milestones I wanted to see. But since I had planned for succession, like Moses, those goals would be met with or without me.

HELP WANTED: SUCCESSOR

Let's look at some of the ways in which Moses raised up Joshua to lead the Israelites into the promised land. Deuteronomy 34:10–12 tells us that Moses was unique, rare, powerful, and successful. He had all of the qualities of a great leader, but early on, he began to pour energy into and raise up Joshua.

What are the characteristics that Joshua had that we need to look for in the next generation of leaders?

The first and perhaps most important quality is *patience*. Joshua had been Moses's assistant since his youth. Most people are more than willing to sign up for a corner office, a nice title, and a hefty paycheck, but to be an assistant for years…that's a big ask.

We should understand, as Moses did, that making good decisions in stressful times, persevering through pain, and understanding the responsibility of leadership takes time. Whether it's *The Karate Kid* from the 1980s, or one of today's DC or Marvel superheroes, it's clear that heroism is learned over time, and dedication is what makes leaders successful. While there are lots of people who may ask you to mentor them, there are only a few who will be patient enough to truly be mentored.

Second, Joshua's *loyalty* allowed his relationship with Moses to grow over time, as Moses was willing to trust and teach him. In Numbers 11:26–28, when Eldad and Medad started to prophesy in the camp, Joshua's first instinct was to urge Moses to tell them to stop. He was afraid that they might undermine his mentor's leadership. While Moses ultimately knew these men were not a threat, Joshua's impulse to go directly to him with his warning revealed his respect and commitment. Loyalty isn't always easy to define, but it is a necessary quality in those you choose to lead.

Third, Joshua was *hungry for opportunity*. He and Moses "*climbed up the mountain of God*" (Exodus 24:13). This wasn't an easy journey; there was no horse, donkey, camel, or cable car to take them to the top. Yet Joshua jumped at the chance to go. He didn't complain or wonder why no one else had to undergo this climb. Remember, Joshua had spent months traveling with this group of folks who did a whole lot of complaining. His willingness to take advantage of every opportunity led to experiences that gave him the wisdom and insight to lead the Israelites into the promised land.

Patience, loyalty, and a hunger for opportunity—these are the characteristics Moses saw in Joshua that led him to begin training the young man who would eventually become his successor. Moses's legacy wasn't diminished by Joshua's success. In fact, it's exactly that ability to identify, train, and empower his successor that led many to believe that Moses is the greatest leader who ever lived. Now that is quite a legacy.

TRAINING DAY

> *IF I WERE A YOUNG COACH TODAY, I WOULD BE*
> *EXTREMELY CAREFUL IN SELECTING ASSISTANTS.*
> —*COACH JOHN WOODEN*

The late John Wooden was the head basketball coach of the UCLA Bruins from 1949 to 1975. In his twenty-seven seasons, his record was a remarkable 316-68. Many people, including me, consider Wooden to be the greatest college basketball coach to ever put on a whistle. But Coach Wooden was more interested in building great young men than great basketball players, and his philosophy of the *pyramid of success* extends far beyond the court. His wisdom is critical to my personal mentorship playbook.

Wooden was also a deeply spiritual man, and he used his strong Christian faith paired with the discipline of basketball to build strong players and individuals. In developing your successor, what's in your playbook? Over decades of training people, I have done things right, and I have messed up spectacularly. But here's what is in my playbook, along with some backup from Coach Wooden. I hope it is helpful for you. Let's do this!

+ *Check your ego at the door.* Wooden believed, "The main ingredient of stardom is the rest of the team." The Israelites never stopped complaining, and there will be those on your team who will also complain. Not everyone you train and mentor will make it to the next level, and this may lead to jealousy, gossip, and negative chatter. Expect it and ignore it!

+ *Give your people opportunities to both succeed and fail.* In Wooden's words, "If you're not making mistakes, then you're not doing anything. I'm positive that a doer makes mistakes." Joshua was just an assistant, but Aaron and Hur were elders. If you give yourself enough time to train your successor, you have plenty of chances to allow them to perform. Make decisions. They may fail or not do everything exactly as you would, but these are opportunities for them to learn.

+ *Spend time with your people and get to know them as just that—people.* "I talked to the players and tried to make them aware of what was good and bad, but I didn't try to run their lives," Wooden said. I think of Hal Mayor, a former executive pastor at Potential Church. Before he would hire anyone, he would meet them for an activity that had nothing to do with the job. Whether they went on a boat ride, played racquetball, or had a meal together, Mayor would try to understand who they were outside of the standard interview environment. Look for those on your team who are open to any chance of spending time with you. When you ask them to lunch, to volunteer on a weekend, or toss a ball around, do they say yes? And, by the way, do you enjoy their company?

+ *Teach the why, not just the what.* I believe, as Wooden did, that teaching "contributes more to the future of our society than any other single profession." My dad didn't just hand me a wrench; he showed me why he needed it and how to use it. Explain to your staff, your kids, or your team *why* you are doing something—whether it's scheduling a meeting, saving money, or cooking dinner—not just what needs to be done. And see who absorbs it!

+ *Empowerment is a process.* "It takes time to create excellence. If it could be done quickly, more people would do it," Wooden said. So empower your people, but don't abandon them.

In Exodus 17, Moses commands Joshua to fight the army of Amalek, but assures him that he will oversee him from the top of a hill, holding up the staff of God, with Aaron and Hur to help support him if needed:

> *As long as Moses held up the staff in his hand, the Israelites had the advantage. But whenever he dropped his hand, the Amalekites gained the advantage. Moses' arms soon became so tired he could no longer hold them up. So Aaron and Hur found a stone for him to sit on. Then they stood on each side of Moses, holding up his hands. So his hands held steady until sunset. As a result, Joshua overwhelmed the army of Amalek in battle.* (Exodus 17:11–13)

Moses empowers Joshua by saying, "You choose who's going to fight. This is your team." (See Exodus 17:9.) But he doesn't add, "I'll be in my tent." Instead, Moses stays engaged. And you'll notice that as long as he keeps his hands up, the Israelites are victorious, but when his hands come down, the enemy gains. Joshua is empowered, but he isn't alone. He doesn't question what Moses asks him to do because he knows Moses and the Lord will continue to support him. Empowerment is a process.

The naked truth is that your journey is about so much more than just you. You can use people along the journey to build a successful brand. You can use the journey to success as an opportunity to build successful people. The decision is yours, but don't wait too long to make it. Your legacy depends on it!

MATERIAL POSSESSIONS, WINNING SCORES, AND GREAT REPUTATIONS ARE MEANINGLESS IN THE EYES OF THE LORD, BECAUSE HE KNOWS WHAT WE REALLY ARE AND THAT IS ALL THAT MATTERS.
—COACH JOHN WOODEN

WHY MOSES, NOT JOSHUA, WINS MVP

You might be wondering, "Well, if Joshua is the one who brought the Israelites into the promised land, why don't we talk about *him* more often? Why doesn't he get a Technicolor movie, with a burly Charlton Heston playing him? Why isn't *he* the focus of this very book instead of Moses?"

In his fantastic guide, *The 21 Irrefutable Laws of Leadership*,[20] one of my favorite business mentors, John C. Maxwell, writes, "A leader's lasting value is measured by succession."

Nowhere is this more starkly illustrated than in the story of Moses and Joshua—for better and for worse. Because even though Joshua displayed great leadership in leading the Israelites into the promised land, he did not invest in anyone to succeed *him*. Sadly, we learn:

> *Joshua son of Nun, the servant of the LORD, died at the age of 110. They buried him in the land he had been allocated, at Timnath-serah in the hill country of Ephraim, north of Mount Gaash. After that generation died, another generation grew up who did not acknowledge the LORD or remember the mighty things he had done for Israel.*
> (Judges 2:8–10)

The Lord was disappointed by this generation of Israelites, who worshipped false gods and diluted the legacy of Moses and Joshua. The Lord fought against them and even allowed raiders to steal their possessions. (See Judges 2:11–15.) As Coach Wooden warned, "Failing to prepare is preparing to fail."

Will you be like Moses, or will you be like Joshua? No one likes to think that they will grow old, retire, die, or be unable to carry forward what they have founded. But leadership is temporary. Plan for your succession, and success will be yours!

---

20. John C. Maxwell, *The 21 Irrefutable Laws of Leadership: Follow Them and People Will Follow You* (Nashville, TN: Thomas Nelson, 1998).

THE PEACE OF SEEKING YOUR POTENTIAL

While lying in that hospital bed with COVID, I was at peace with the idea of dying—but I'm pretty happy that I recovered! That peace stays with me, as does the knowledge that I must make time to continue to develop people, systems, and legacies for the next generation *right now*, each and every day.

I returned home from the hospital after several days, physically diminished but buoyed with emotional and intellectual strength. I was filled with purpose and a renewed sense of my potential. I knew this last chapter would now be better and richer for the experience—and I would have the confidence to complete it. How great is God and how wondrous are His ways!

God is waiting for *you* to unleash your potential, His uncontainable power within you. Nothing is stopping you, so go for it!

> *"For I know the plans I have for you," declares the* Lord, *"plans to prosper you and not to harm you, plans to give you hope and a future."* (Jeremiah 29:11 NIV)

QUESTIONS FOR REFLECTION

What does the phrase "leadership is temporary" mean to you?

Will you be like Moses, or will you be like Joshua? What are three things that you can do right now to plan for your succession, whether it be in your family, your business, your church, or your organization?

What actions, characteristics, and skills do you want to be known for?

What do you want people to remember about the impact you have made on whatever you are leading or on them personally?

BIBLIOGRAPHY

Blanchard, Kenneth. *Leadership and the One Minute Manager.* New York: William Morrow & Co., 1985.

Collins, Jim, and Porras, Jerry I. *Built to Last: Successful Habits of Visionary Companies.* New York: Harper Business, 1997.

Collins, Jim. *Good to Great: Why Some Companies Make the Leap and Others Don't.* New York: Harper Collins, 2001.

Collins, Jim. *How the Mighty Fall: And Why Some Companies Never Give In.* New York: Harper Collins, 2009.

Colson, Charles. *Tough Questions about God, Faith, and Life: Answers to the Difficult Questions Teens Ask.* Carol Stream, IL: Tyndale House Publishers, 2006.

Covey, Stephen R. *The 8th Habit: From Effectiveness to Greatness.* New York: Free Press, 2005.

Gladwell, Malcolm. *Outliers: The Story of Success.* New York: Little, Brown and Company, 2008.

Godin, Seth. *Linchpin: Are You Indispensable?* New York: Portfolio, 2011.

Goodwin, Doris Kearns. *Team of Rivals: The Political Genius of Abraham Lincoln.* New York: Simon & Schuster, 2006.

Groeschel, Craig. *Chazown: Discover and Pursue God's Purpose for Your Life.* Colorado Springs, CO: Multonomah, 2017.

Lencioni, Patrick M. *Getting Naked: A Business Fable About Shedding the Three Fears That Sabotage Client Loyalty.* New York: John Wiley & Sons, 2009.

Maxwell, John C. *Developing the Leader Within You.* Nashville, TN: Thomas Nelson, 2005.

Maxwell, John C. *The 21 Irrefutable Laws of Leadership: Follow Them and People Will Follow You.* Nashville, TN: Thomas Nelson, 1998.

Morgan, Robert J. *The Red Sea Rules: 10 God-Given Strategies for Difficult Times.* Nashville, TN: Thomas Nelson, 2014.

Peters, Thomas J., and Waterman, Robert H. *In Search of Excellence: Lessons from America's Best-Run Companies.* New York: Harper & Row, 1982.

Pressfield, Steven. *The Legend of Bagger Vance: A Novel of Golf and the Game of Life.* New York: William Morrow, 1995.

Southerland, Dan. *Transitioning: Leading Your Church Through Change.* Grand Rapids, MI: Zondervan, 2002.

Warren, Rick. *The Purpose Driven Life: What on Earth Am I Here For?* Grand Rapids, MI: Zondervan, 2002.

ABOUT THE AUTHOR

For over twenty years, Pastor Troy Gramling has led Potential Church, a fast-growing church with more than 20,000 members at locations in the United States and Latin America. A former teacher and college basketball coach, Troy is passionate about partnering with people to reach their God-given potential to impact the world for good.

A former teacher and college basketball coach, Troy excels in leadership development and is well known for his creative and unexpected teaching experiences, such as living in an all-glass house with his wife Stephanie and collecting thousands of turkeys for a food drive using the slogan, "Flip Us a Bird!"

Before moving to South Florida, Troy and Steph planted a church in Northeast Arkansas that began with nine people in a living room. This church became one of the fastest growing churches in Arkansas.

Troy received his BSE in Secondary Education and Teaching from Arkansas State University and an associate's degree in coaching from Williams Baptist College.

Troy and Steph live in Fort Lauderdale, Florida. They have three grown children, Tyler, Carson, and Baylee, all of whom serve with them in ministry.